AUGUST KLEINZAHLER

CUTTY, ONE ROCK

August Kleinzahler was born in Jersey City in 1949.
He is the author of ten books of poems and was
awarded the 2004 Griffin Poetry Prize for *The Strange
Hours Travelers Keep*. He lives in San Francisco.

ALSO BY AUGUST KLEINZAHLER

The Strange Hours Travelers Keep

Live from the Hong Kong Nile Club:
Poems 1975–1990

Green Sees Things in Waves

Red Sauce, Whiskey and Snow

Like Cities, Like Storms

Earthquake Weather

Storm over Hackensack

A Calendar of Airs

The Sausage Master of Minsk: Poems

CUTTY, ONE ROCK

AUGUST KLEINZAHLER

Cutty, One Rock

LOW CHARACTERS

AND STRANGE PLACES,

GENTLY EXPLAINED

FARRAR, STRAUS AND GIROUX

NEW YORK

Farrar, Straus and Giroux
19 Union Square West, New York 10003

Copyright © 2004, 2005 by August Kleinzahler
All rights reserved
Distributed in Canada by Douglas & McIntyre Ltd.
Printed in the United States of America
Published in 2004 by Farrar, Straus and Giroux
First paperback edition, 2005

Earlier versions of most of these essays appeared in
Areté, *The London Review of Books*, *Poetry*, *San Diego
Reader*, *Sulfur*, and *The Threepenny Review*.

Grateful acknowledgment is made for permission
to reprint the following previously published material:
Excerpt from *Lucretius: The Way Things Are*, translated by Rolfe
Humphries, reproduced courtesy of Indiana University Press.
Excerpt from "H," from *Rimbaud: Collected Poems*, translated by
Oliver Bernard, reproduced courtesy of Penguin Books Ltd.

Library of Congress Control Number: 2005935231
ISBN-13: 978-0-374-53018-1
ISBN-10: 0-374-53018-1

Designed by Quemadura

www.fsgbooks.com

1 3 5 7 9 10 8 6 4 2

FOR MR. WOOSTER, WHO, WITH THE
HELP OF HIS RIGHT SHOE, TAUGHT ME
TO DIAGRAM A SENTENCE IN 1962

CONTENTS

Part One

Part Two

Part Three

Part Four

Part One

THE DOG, THE FAMILY:

A HOUSEHOLD TALE

It was the dog who raised me. Oh, the others came and went with their nurturing gestures and concerns, but it was the dog on whose ear I teethed and who watched me through countless hours with the sagacity and bearing of a Ugandan tribal chief.

You can see him straining at the collar as my mother, dressed to the nines, first introduced him to me, freshly home from the hospital, lying across the nurse's lap, almost afloat, like an early Renaissance Christ child. You can see the muscles in his shoulders and neck. Perhaps he would have eaten me right then had I not been smelling of Mother, who I must say looks very pretty there in profile, probably about to head off to her Shakespeare club or into the city to see Paul Scofield in *Lear*, or something along those lines. Mother was very keen on Shakespeare, you see.

Going through the old photo albums you will find pictures of me in various stages of growing up, surrounded by the family: father, mother, sister, brother. But please notice, it is the dog at my side, seated upright, proudly displaying the musculature of his thick chest and the flame of white fur that ornamented it. I am his charge, the rest of them bit players.

Not so much a Romulus-and-Remus situation as my having a guardian, a sort of dog uncle, rearing me in lieu of parents.

Actually, the dog looked very human, rather more so than one or two other members of the family. I had forgotten just how extreme was his facial resemblance to a human being until recently, when I showed my ladylove, Tarischa, an old photograph of the dog and me on the front stoop. Her eyes grew very large, then she began gagging.

We called him Granny or Grand, shortened from Twenty Grand, the famous racehorse after whom he was named. Father bought him on sale. He bought everything on sale. Grand was a boxer, purebred, but one of his ears was wrong; it didn't set up properly. And his right eye dripped. He also had a skin condition, something like mange but untreatable. Father got him for peanuts, really: a treasure, if you looked past certain cosmetic flaws.

Granny was a killer, but only when off the leash out of doors. He killed the chihuahua next door and Ernie Middel- hauser's dog, Jo-Jo. He seldom attacked humans, only dogs, male dogs. Female dogs brought out his romantic side. You see, if you weren't careful when you opened the front or back door, he would shoot by you or between your legs and be gone for days. Eventually, he'd turn up hungry, looking a bit haggard. Father would kick him for a while until he tired of the exercise, and Granny would take it stoically, without growling or baring his teeth, only looking back at Father now and then with an ugly sneer.

I did miss him when he was off on one of his adventures, left alone with my toy soldiers and the cartoon shows of television's infancy. I recall one where a clown—I seem to remember his name was Cocoa—jumped out of an inkwell and made some difficulty for his creator. Cocoa was animated, the creator not: this provoked my imagination. After some difficulty, the creator always succeeded in getting Cocoa back in the bottle. There are certainly metaphors and allegories aplenty here if you go in for such things. Regardless, the dog would eventually return and we would pick up where we left off, no questions asked, no pouting or recriminations.

It's not as if the rest of the family weren't around. Father was at work, quite naturally, and Mother shopping, or perhaps at her Shakespeare club, which met on alternate Tuesdays. My brother would have been in the basement, at work on a model airplane, getting himself stoned senseless on glue fumes. Or if not in the basement, then in the apple tree, seeing how far he could get out on a limb before it snapped.

My sister lived in the attic. It was not such a bad thing to have her always up there, as she had Father's unpredictable disposition. Well, not always: she would occasionally come down to gnaw the meat off the steak bone we were ordered to save for her. Oh, and there were the suitors. My sister had an hourglass figure and a pixie hairdo. She favored very stupid boys with dodgy backgrounds and convertibles.

Otherwise, she read her Latin in the attic or, when saturated with Ovid, would play her rock-and-roll seventy-eights on her portable. She played "The Naughty Lady of Shady Lane" repeatedly, hundreds of times, for months on end. She would dance to this and other tunes: *thump, thump, thump*. No one in the family was particularly graceful, excepting the dog and, to a certain extent, me, having modeled my own movements on the dog's. My brother was not graceful but had a primitive athleticism, as I imagine the young Tecumseh or Cochise must have had, an athleticism given almost wholly over to mayhem. My brother was not unlike the dog in the behavior he evinced out of the house. Nor did Father receive my brother much differently from the dog when he'd stagger home at last with his assorted wounds and bills incurred.

My sister spent so much time in the attic with her Latin that she broke the record for A pluses at the local high school and went off to Smith College after her junior year to study Latin in the Big Leagues of American Higher Education. Such intellectual prowess was unheard of at this particular high school and my sister became a legend there, her name synonymous with braininess. The only other equivalent celebrity from that high school during that time was the fellow who wrote the hit song "Flying Purple People Eater," and there might even have been some challenge as to the song's *real* authorship.

Mother didn't like children, least of all her own, and me least among them. I was unplanned, an accident, a misfortune. You see, Mother and Father had taken the Fishblatts, their friends from around the corner, out to dinner, and everybody got quite drunk. That had been my parents' plan: to get the Fishblatts drunk. It seems the Fishblatts were making ready for a divorce, which signaled no more impromptu get-togethers only a hop, skip, and jump away. I suppose the plan was that when the appropriate level of drunkenness

6

was achieved, there would be a series of ribald and stoical jokes about the imperfect union of marriage, hoots of exasperation, and unbridled guffaws, and the Fishblatts would stagger home, enjoy an amorous reconciliation of robust proportion, and resign themselves to being stuck with one another for the duration, a circumstance relieved from time to time by visits with my parents.

Well, now, it didn't turn out like that at all. The Fishblatts sobered up straightaway and got divorced. Mother became pregnant with me, years after she'd convinced herself she'd beaten that particular rap.

My appearance on the scene was unwelcome enough, but it turned out that I looked like the dog. I am not suggesting that Mother had been impregnated by Granny, not at all. You see, if Mother had only listened to her own mother and averted her eyes from the dog during the term of her pregnancy, it was said, this unhappy result might have been avoided. Nanny Farbisseneh, a tiny, dour creature originally from a bog outside of Kiev, who, when she spoke at all, issued terse commands in a broken English that drifted erratically into a goulash of Russian, Ukrainian, and Yiddish, held powerful, almost frightening influence over her three daughters, of whom Mother was the youngest. In the presence of Nanny, Mother and my two aunts were like zombified servant girls, oblivious of their own wants and those of their respective families.

Nanny Farbisseneh disapproved of dogs, and held a dim view of males of any species, so you see, a male dog, especially one with Granny's imperfections, could succeed only in eliciting her unalloyed revulsion. But despite Nanny Far's injunctions, Mother not only continued to look at the dog but gazed lovingly into his eyes (the right one caked with discharge) for hours on end. Mother, it turns out, loved four-legged creatures, both cloven and hoofed, and, without exception, even the most vicious and recalcitrant, they adored her, not least of all Grand. True, Mother fed the dog and saw to the removal of his feces, but Granny's love for Mother went far beyond this natural bond: the dog was in love with Mother, a situation that did not go unnoticed by Father, who routinely attacked the dog, either with his right foot or a rolled-up copy of *The Atlantic Monthly* brought down sharply on the dog's black, concertinaed snout.

So Mother, who seldom, if ever, disobeyed Nanny Far, in this instance made an egregious exception, one that she would rue and suffer to be daily reminded of for years and years. In fact, so considerable was her distress at having been delivered of this curious whelp that not a week after my birth both my parents disappeared to Guatemala for a fortnight, presumably to console one another, divert themselves with Mayan figurines, rain forests, cloudy fermented beverages made from tubers—whatever one does in such places. But in truth, knowing Father, Guatemala was probably that season's cheapest ticket. And Mother really, really wanted to get the hell out of Dodge.

My resemblance to the dog was not my only embarrassment to the family. I had a thick Czech accent as well, at least until the age of seven or so, when Father let our housekeeper, Christine, go. If memory serves, because she asked for a small raise after many years of devoted service.

Christine was a round, bosomy, gray-haired Czech woman, grandmotherly, if you will, but in the nice movie-and-
storybook way as opposed to the Nanny Far way. Christine
smelled of dough and fresh laundry. She loved me and had
me entirely convinced I was the singular joy in her life, although I knew she had a son of her own. In the evenings,
Christine would cook deep-fried potatoes, the smell of which
was an enchantment. The memory of those potatoes stirs me
to this day. It was an aroma of such pleasurable intensity
that it seemed of another world and time, perhaps a subterranean wood-paneled beer hall–cum–restaurant somewhere in Bratislava, where officers, business leaders, and
ladies of fashion would congregate a century earlier, taking
refuge from the harsh elements and sustenance in the
hearty, blissfully aromatic fare.

Then, after Christine had cleaned up, she would go home
to her no-good, delinquent son, her three-room, cabbagey
shithole, and watch *The Joe Franklin Show*, or some trash
of that sort, like the ignorant bohunk she was. But to me,
Christine was maternal beneficence, pleasure and abun-
dance, my anti-Mother. Years later, as an adult, I would live
with a young Czech woman, Canadian-Czech, and suck my
thumb till it was raw as I watched her cook pierogi, chicken
paprikash, her special Bohemian cookies. Then, when we
were done eating, I'd lick her breasts while we copulated for
hours, all the time thinking of Christine's tattersall apron
and the smell of her fried potatoes from across the years.

When Christine had left, Mother took it into her head to take
a more active role in the rearing of her youngest child, me.
The dog was sent whimpering to the den. It was just Mother

and me at the kitchen table. I remember the moment very well, to this day. She clearly had plans for me, and her appraising, contemptuous look augured nothing good, at least insofar as I was concerned.

"It's back to the good ol' U. S. of A. for you, babykins," she said to me. "Let's lose the Kafka accent. It's giving your father and me the creeps, and your brother and sister are too embarrassed to bring home any of their friends. You're going to speak like an American child and act like an American child. And while you're at it, wipe the *schmutz* off your chin."

Had I forgotten what I told Mother at that particular point, her tittering rendition of it over the years would have been more than adequate in refreshing my memory: "I vont you should take a valk in dee voods and a beeg, bad volf eat you all whup!" That one really cracked her pits. "You really are the limit," she said mirthlessly, shaking her head in dismay. I could hear the dog whining piteously from behind the closed parlor doors.

Mother explained to me that if I didn't come around, and in a hurry, she'd make me take a job in Uncle Ja-Ja's factory, blocking hats. Uncle Ja-Ja was Nanny Far's little brother, although he, too, was ancient. He resembled an engorged frog with thick, black-rimmed glasses, and smelled of gherkins. Ja-Ja was always looking for cheap labor—child, adult, no matter—and surely would have jumped at the idea, but it was Great-Aunt Duhnny, the final authority among the Kiev bog contingent, who put her foot down. "Dog-boy go to school like ordinary child," she said, and that was that.

Father worked and read the paper. Children and child rearing, in his view, belonged to the realm of the female, and in my case the dog. The children were Mother's bailiwick. His job was to make money, then lose it, make it again, and so on, except when he was reading the paper, which was fillled with information on how to make money, along with insights into the perils of how it might be lost.

Money and the record of its activity was not Father's only interest. He had a fascination with what he called "antiquities," or at least what they cost. In particular, he liked bodhisattvas, religious statuary from the Orient of sacred figures like Avalokitesvara, Manjusri, Kshitigarbha. Why a man of almost no formal education (having been repeatedly thrown out of school for antisocial behavior) should cotton to these small sculptures of holy beings who seek Buddhahood through the practice of perfect virtues, well . . . Regardless, the house looked like a Chinese souvenir shop, which was a terrible cross for Mother to bear. A frightful snob about such things, Mother, who cherished a Todd Haynes look in domestic interiors, would sit there on the living-room sofa, smoking her Salems, and, regarding the clutter of sacred figures, say, "Just look at all that shit," shaking her head disconsolately.

Fortunately, or unfortunately, for Mother, Father, like those primeval forests that spontaneously autocombust every century or two to get rid of old growth and make room for new, every few months would go berserk and destroy everything in the house, invariably heading first for the bodhisattvas. I can only speculate in hindsight how many dozens of Avalokitesvaras (the bodhisattva of compassion, known as Kuan-yin in China) Father cracked over the mantelpiece.

As for the rest of us during these episodes, led by Mother,

and with the dog bringing up the rear, we would retreat to the upstairs bathroom and lock ourselves in until it was evident the storm had blown itself out. It was not unpleasant to be in that small room with the rest of them for the fifteen or twenty minutes it took Father to "clear the brush out" downstairs. I seldom got to visit with my older siblings at such close quarters, and Mother seemed a veritable font of drolleries on these occasions. The dog was in good humor as well and relieved not to be on the other side of the door. When the crashing, grunts, and gargled imprecations subsided, we would proceed single file, in the exact order we had retreated, downstairs, where, inevitably, we'd find Father seated there in the living room, staring rather pensively at the rubble.

Years later, my psychologist girlfriend Clarissa would say to me, "Dog, has anyone ever suggested to you that you're rather, um, *labile*?"

Fucking bitch ... But turns out she didn't mean what I thought.

The years passed. One day Father looked up from his paper and asked Mother where their two older children had gone; he hadn't seen them in a while. "They've been away at college for years, darling," she told him. The dog was getting on as well. I'd try to engage him in our customary frolic, but he'd only look up at me miserably, his dark jowls spread across the carpet.

In fact, Granny didn't age at all gracefully. He had never been what one would think of as a good-smelling creature, given as he was to flatulence and halitosis, along with an indefinable but distinctly unwholesome smell emanating from his diseased skin. It was not at all uncommon for the dog to puke up something he'd gotten into, and the house really was beginning to smell like a doggie vomitorium. Other than that, he slept, occasionally breaking wind or struggling to his feet to pee at the base of this chair or that. Toward the very end, he'd even gone off his horsemeat.

One day I came home from school to find Mother weeping at the foot of the hall stairs. It was a startling spectacle. I'd have been no less astonished if she'd taken wing and commenced doing the loop-the-loops over the house; or had I encountered Grand up on his hind legs singing "Que Sera, Sera" in a tremulous countertenor. Uh-oh, where was the dog? Even at this advanced stage in his decline he would probably have roused himself and staggered over. The dog would have found Mother's weeping no less peculiar and alarming than I.

So it was, staring at Mother with the curiosity and skepticism of an art historian or scientist dispatched by a museum to check out the phenomenon of "the weeping Madonna" in a dank little Italian church buried among the cypresses of some hill town, that I realized the dog was gone. Kaput. And with that realization came another: still a child, I was alone in the world; but far worse, alone with Mother and Father.

TOO BAD ABOUT MRS. FERRI

On a fine late October afternoon in 1957 I came home from school to a great commotion at the foot of the block where we lived. TV trucks and news reporters were clustered at the gates to the long drive leading up to Albert Anastasia's enormous Spanish Mission–style home. The Palisades section of Fort Lee, New Jersey, then as now, was a sleepy, leafy enclave overlooking the Upper West Side, a mile or so across the Hudson.

My mother came out the front door of our house, walked up to me, knelt down, and said, "Augie, Gloriana's daddy got very, very sick, and Gloriana and her mommy are going to have to go away for a while, so Gloriana won't be coming over to play." Gloriana's daddy sure did get sick. Albert Anastasia, head of Murder Incorporated and capo of the Mangano family, had been assassinated that morning at ten-twenty while getting a shave at the Park Sheraton Hotel on Seventh Avenue.

The Gallo brothers made the hit: Joseph, "Crazy Joe"; Larry; and Albert, "Kid Blast." They were accompanied by an ugly little torpedo named Joseph "Joe Jelly" Giorelli, who finished the job with a bullet to the back of Anastasia's head. These four were the aces of Joseph Profaci's hit squad. But the order had come from higher up, from Vito Genovese himself. Anastasia was whacked because he was too dangerous. His appetite for killing had made him reckless and a liability, and the other mobsters had called him (behind his back, of course) "the Mad Hatter."

It wasn't very considerate of him to kill our plumber, Mr. Ferri. Reliable plumbers are hard to come by; they were then, they are now. Mr. Ferri was Anastasia's plumber as well, and he must have seen something he wasn't supposed to see. The Feds put Mr. Ferri and his wife in the witness protection program, down south in some Miami suburb. Ha, ha, ha. Who the fuck did they think they were dealing with, huh? Too bad about Mrs. Ferri. But on balance my folks found Anastasia an exemplary neighbor. He minded his own business and was very polite when their paths crossed. I'm not sure when that was, given that Anastasia tended to keep odd hours and spent a lot of time in his Oldsmobile luxury sedan going back and forth between Jersey and New York, driven by his most trusted bodyguard, Anthony "Tough Tony" Coppola. "Courtly" was how my parents described Anastasia.

I don't suppose it was Tough Tony who brought little Gloriana to my parents' house every day and babysat for the two of us while my mother went off shopping or visited friends. It was some other affectless gorilla with a shoulder holster. "Play-a nice, children," he would say if things started going to hell in the sandpit. Apart from Gloriana and her mommy, it was my mother who was most saddened by Anastasia's untimely death. For with him went the best babysitter on earth. Mother knew that if anything, anything at all, happened to either of us, the babysitter would have his dick shot off.

New Jersey was famous for gangsters, way ahead of *The Sopranos*, and Fort Lee most famous of all. Like Walt Whitman before them, a number of enterprising souls had come over to the "Left Bank" from Brooklyn. Guys like Willie Moretti, Tony Bender, and Joe Adonis, né Doto, who took the name Adonis on account of he was so fucking good-looking. The "Al Capone of New Jersey" was another good-looking guy named Longy Zwillman, whose favorite party trick was to produce from his wallet a pubic hair belonging to Jean Harlow, with whom he'd had a hot affair.

The local headquarters for these men was an Italian restaurant called Duke's Place in Cliffside Park, the next town south from Fort Lee. My folks went there quite often because it was close-by and the food was good. That is, until my mother, who is given to irrepressible asides about people's appearance and speculation about their personal lives, remarked to my father one evening at Duke's, "How old could that little blonde number be over there with those two hoods?" My mother does not have a small voice, and this met with a poor, but not fatal, response. My father was not given to asides but tended in his younger days to grow very agitated in restaurants when he felt the service was lackadaisical. One evening at another local hood joint, probably Joe's Elbow Room, my parents hadn't even received a menu after sitting there for twenty minutes. The place was empty aside from a plenary council of silk suits involved in a confab over some ziti. Having enjoyed many episodes of my father's behavior in such situations, I shudder to think what might have happened next. Fortunately one of those silk suits belonged to Mr. Anastasia. The folks were served with remarkable dispatch, and the pasta was al dente, as my father liked it.

Fort Lee was, in those days, a vivid little town, not the usual American suburb. My family lived at the southern end, a couple of blocks from Cliffside Park and only three blocks from one of the largest amusement parks in America, where for six months of the year you could hear the screams of people riding the Whip or the Cyclone, the giant roller coaster.

At the north end of town was the George Washington Bridge, and just above the bridge a famous hood nightclub called the Riviera, which always booked star entertainers and put on gala floor shows. But it was more famous for its plush gambling casino at the back, the Marine Room, which was off-limits to ordinary patrons. The Marine Room was run by the Zwillman-Moretti syndicate. One of the star acts at the Riviera was Frank Sinatra, a skinny Jersey boy from down the road in Hoboken. Moretti took a shine to Sinatra, whom he probably first saw perform as a singer-waiter at a little roadhouse called the Rustic Cabin in the next town north, Englewood. He helped the youngster get some band dates. Later on, Sinatra signed with Tommy Dorsey, became a star, and then wanted out of his contract. Dorsey wasn't having any of it, however, at least not until Moretti jammed a gun down his throat, petitioning the band leader to exercise reason and good judgment.

Twenty years ago, shortly after I came to live in San Francisco, my cousin Seymour, who lived in Mill Valley and for a time had been Sinatra's agent, or one of them, took me to dinner at the Fairmont Hotel on Nob Hill. Seymour was showbiz and liked to make a flashy impression. After dinner he made me drink a sambuca with a coffee bean in it. He told me this was what classy guys drink. I asked him if Sinatra was Mob. Without missing a beat, Seymour laughed and said, "Are you kidding? Frankie's a pussycat; he couldn't hurt a fly, even if he tried. He just likes to pretend he's a gangster." Which is presumably what he was doing in 1946 when he posed in Havana for a photo op with his arm around Lucky Luciano's shoulder. Another nice picture shows him with Carlo Gambino, who was the intermediary between Vito Genovese and Joseph Profaci in the Anastasia hit: Frankie-boy is smiling in his dressing room at the Premier Theater in Westchester, New York, next to Carlo and the hit man (later informer) Jimmy "the Weasel" Fratianno and three other hoods later convicted and sentenced for fraud and skimming the theater's box office.

Frank, who was a good son, bought a lovely home for his mother, Dolly, in Fort Lee. I'm sure Dolly enjoyed her stay, even if she missed some of the old crowd from her local ward in Hoboken, where she did quite a few favors for the local big shots. Fort Lee in those days was about 98 percent Italian. There were a few Jewish families, like mine, a couple of Greek families, an Irish family, an Armenian family, but everyone else was Southern Italian. You might as well have been in Palermo, except the buildings were newer.

David Chase, the *Sopranos* creator, grew up in Essex County. Fort Lee is Bergen County, but never you mind. I played as a child with Tony Soprano and his pals, if you can imagine them as eight-year-olds. During recess and the lunch hour the schoolyard at No. 4 Elementary School in

Fort Lee was like a theme park for Tourette's syndrome. There is a scene in *Scarface*, the movie by Brian De Palma (born Newark, New Jersey, Essex County), in which Al Pacino is sitting in the bath, cranked up on coke and launched on a rant, when his ice-goddess new wife, played by Michelle Pfeiffer, says something like, "Are you capable of finishing a whole sentence without repeating the word 'fuck'?" Sometimes there was a bit of *va fungule*. Other popular terms of abuse were "faggot" and "douche." The use of the latter is somewhat mysterious: it was directed exclusively at other males and no one had any idea what a douche bag was. It was also bellowed out in a particular fashion, in order to achieve maximum release for the diphthong. Duckie Juliano was a master of this art. One time I called someone a son of a bitch, which must have sounded preposterously foreign and Noël Coward–like. All activity ceased, and I was viciously assaulted by Tommy Grumulia and Anthony Delvecchio. Boys are formed by the playgrounds they come from. Ours was violent, noisy, and profane, somewhat operatic in the Italian manner. But there were no guns or knives and no one ever got seriously hurt, except when Louis Boccia tore off most of his ear after running too close to the cyclone fence during a game of salugi. But it got sewed back on, almost like new.

Not long after Mrs. Anastasia and Gloriana went away, the big house was bought by Buddy Hackett, a fat little funnyman who had a successful TV and lounge act. He looked rather cherubic, in a greasy way, with his button nose and chubby cheeks, and this allowed him to get away with stories and jokes that were quite blue for the time. Also, he had a peculiar way of speaking, almost a speech defect. He had a thick Brooklyn accent and his voice seemed to live moistly in the back of his throat, the effect much compounded by what seemed to be marbles or acorns or jelly beans in his mouth. Each word or phrase had a messy, difficult birth. His pièce de résistance was his Chinese waiter routine, in which he put a rubber band over his head and face so his eyes narrowed like a Chinese. In the sketch Hackett took an order from a table at a restaurant, and when it was time for dessert, he would intone, in his Brooklyn-Chinese accent, "Okay, who the wise guy with the kumquat?"

After dinner one night my parents told me to go get Buddy Hackett's autograph. My parents had no interest in Buddy Hackett's autograph. They hardly ever watched TV and were convinced I was mildly retarded because I did. No, they were sending me forth, in their endearing Jersey City way, as a trial balloon.

I had never been to the big house. Gloriana and the gorilla always came to me. But I knocked at the door. A frightened, bewildered Hispanic maid in uniform opened it. I gave my little talk: "I'm Augie Kleinzahler from down the street and I would like Mr. Hackett's autograph, please." The maid, looking stricken, disappeared, and next up was a woman I took to be Mrs. Hackett. She said something mildly discouraging but I didn't budge, knowing better than to return home without a result. At which point Mrs. Hackett disappeared.

I immediately registered the cause of their apprehension when the famous entertainer himself came waddling to the front door. He was barely taller than I was, and I was seven years old. He was red-faced and breathing moistly and with some difficulty, like a toy bulldog on a sultry day. "Whuh da you want, kid?" he asked in one of America's most distinctive voices. I identified myself, told him where I lived, and asked for his autograph. He glared at me, incredulous, for a few moments (I could sense the wife and maid cowering inside) and said, "Fuck you, kid; talk to my agent!" and slammed the door in my face.

I stood there briefly, considering my options, then turned and walked down the long driveway. It was a pleasant summer evening, fragrant, the maples in leaf and the air filled with cries of terror from the nearby amusement park. I found my parents where I had left them, on the back porch, reading. My mother looked up from her book and smiled. "Well?" she said. "He said, 'Fuck you, kid; talk to my agent.'" My father went back to his book. My mother, for what seemed a long time, stared at me over her reading glasses. "Well," she asked, "did you at least get his agent's name and phone number?"

EAST/WEST VARIATIONS

There's a window, thirty-six hours or so, not even, when traveling by air between places, places where you've lived for a long time. After you've landed and into the next day, perhaps the evening—then you begin to lose it. It goes very quickly, decaying like a tone in the air. But for a while, inside that window, you're hyperawake. I'm talking about light, scale, smell, all of it familiar, but for that short while extending beyond the common registers of the familiar until the buildings, river light, the smell of benzene and tidal flats, what have you, become almost stereoscopic, carrying a taste of the unreal—as if the world had been passed through a solution, cleansed.

I take much pleasure in these hours, perhaps too much. I anticipate them. I savor them afterward and even try to put them to use. I plan my time and movements for when I'll be inside this window. The degree and nature of intensity are not always the same. Even the duration will vary. Like a drug, it can be overpowering, even unpleasant. The heat of combustion depends on atmospheric conditions, internal and external.

Rain is good. It was raining when I took the ferry to Jersey that Sunday afternoon. It's not a long ride, only twelve minutes or so. Heading into New York City in daylight, I en-

22

joy the dense vertical chiaroscuro in front of me, looming larger and larger, and as the ferry closes on it, the sense of sliding into its great maw, of the city pushing in on me. But I like best leaving the city by ferry at night, heading toward the cliffs of Weehawken and the desultory sprays of light. The great lit towers of Midtown rearing up behind as the ferry leaves its slip and heads for the opposite shore never fail to move me.

Places are conditions of mind. They're places, to be sure, but after that initial phase of entry, or re-entry, when you're awake to change and the attendant little spasms of memory and the senses, you're soon anesthetized. You wake up in the place as if you'd never left. It's like visiting your family and almost immediately turning back into the child you were.

The Passaic River drops with considerable force and spectacle some seventy feet at the Great Falls of Paterson. There's a nice picture of it on the cover of William Carlos Williams's book-length poem *Paterson*. The river makes its way through traprock and sandstone to the level plain of the city, continues north to Hawthorne, then reverses itself and begins its southerly flow to Newark Bay, about twenty-five miles through manufacturing and industrial towns and suburbs, places like Garfield, Lyndhurst, Kearny, and Harrison, where it hooks east, then south again under the Pulaski Skyway and into Newark Bay.

These are working towns, low-lying, all dirty brick and clapboard, drab little shopping strips and VFWs and Little League fields: nothing remarkable about them except the cancer rates. You see them as you fly in and out of Newark Airport. And the river flowing through them, picking up effluents from service stations, slaughterhouses, tanneries, chemical plants. People used to drink from the Passaic. In 1881 the Newark Aqueduct Board noted, "Instead of sweet-tasting limpid water, we have a bluish red liquid, disgusting to the taste and smell." And always to the east, the towers of Manhattan across the meadows, partially hidden by the hump of the Palisades, an eroded cross section of a diabase sill hundreds of feet thick and dipping gradually northwest-ward.

The New Jersey character—at least this part of Jersey—is straightforward, plainspoken to the point of bluntness, though not at all unfriendly. The humor is deadpan, ironical, playfully deprecating. It's a beer-and-a-bump kind of place. Affectation is quickly and viscerally registered. There's a swagger, a bluff air of menace that many of the males wear. Sinatra is a caricature of it; Jack Nicholson has it going on as well. Once, after leaving a restaurant in North Beach, here in San Francisco, I gave a panhandler a dollar, a middle-aged black guy with some amusing riff or other.

"Thanks, Jersey," he said, to the great amusement of my companions.

"How did you know I was from Jersey?" I asked.

"Are you kidding?" he said.

I can't tell you how many times I've flown in and out of Newark Airport over the past thirty years. Over the Goethals Bridge and the Kill Van Kull, where Newark Bay feeds into the Narrows of New York Harbor, the "windowed cliffs" of lower Manhattan brilliantly alight as you bank west on the approach to Newark at night. During the day you can see the cloverleafs, storage tanks and freight yards, the shopping centers and clusters of homes. Heading over the western edge of Jersey, you pass over the Great Swamp and the headwaters of the Passaic. We are now at our cruising altitude of thirty-three thousand feet. You are free to unfasten your seat belts and move around the cabin as you wish.

I remember one night I was flying into Newark from the West Coast. It's always night when I land at Newark. I still had that sickness in me from when she left. It seemed to go on for years. The first wave of it nearly did me in.

I don't know how long it had been. I do know we'd already stopped getting together when I came to New York. What a fucking disaster that was. I'd be hemorrhaging up and down Second Avenue as I walked from Astor Place to Twelfth Street. There I'd be at her door with a bottle of vinho verde and blood pouring down my trouser leg. There'd she be, mop in one hand and a pail of disinfectant in the other, like an apprehensive young wife in a 1950s Spic and Span commercial.

That particular evening, the plane made this steep bank toward Jersey, with lower Manhattan, the Twin Towers, and the rest all lit up, and falling away at about a sixty-degree angle, and this horrible sensation passed through me, just horrible—not nausea or any other sort of pain or discomfort with which I was familiar, not even the love agony I'd felt after she went. It was worse than that. I couldn't breathe. I would have groaned or cried out, but nothing was coming out of me. Nothing. There was nothing left in there to come out; that was the problem. When the plane began its steep turn, whatever was holding me together had disappeared out my mouth, like they say your soul does—a little invisible bird fluttering off—when you die.

I had the cab let me off at the foot of the block. I wanted to slow things down a bit, take in the neighborhood. It had been a few years. There were some new, outsize homes built over two lots and extending out to the sidewalk: Greco-Roman fortresses, my father called them. But it was the same sleepy place, only the sound of the rain falling on the canopy of leaves belonging to the maples that lined the street.

There's a very particular afternoon rain light you get in the summer here, that and the smell of the grass and wet pavement. It came over me like a powerful narcotic. I knew it would. Being back after so long away, especially this time of year . . . I was being played like a pipe organ, and with all the stops pulled out: *Cor de nuit, Hautbois, Voix humaine.*

The back door was open. I walked in. Nothing had really changed. I felt like one of those characters in a Dutch painting, "the old burgher's son," returning to the canvas out of which I'd strayed for a time, having lost my way.

My parents were in the living room, entertaining. An out-of-town relation, a retired professor, and his wife had come by to say hello. In truth, they were there to say good-bye. There were copies of my books and publications spread across the coffee table, along with pastries. My father and mother embraced me as if it was nothing out of the ordinary for me to turn up after four years. The cousins glowered, clearly having been brought up to date on the prodigal's unspeakable behavior. I did my best to be cordial, even charming, in an attempt to dispel their low opinion of me. I don't know why I bothered, really. Habit, some vestigial notion of courtesy . . .

As little of my mother as there was left, she looked very nice, almost pretty, a bit like the more elegantly dressed old Chinese women I see in San Francisco from time to time. She's got a touch of Tartar in the eyes, and in her older age seems to favor a vaguely Oriental look: quilted jackets and what looked to be black silk pants.

Even this close to death she remains a clotheshorse. This is even remarked on in her high school yearbook. I told her that her hair looked nice. She apologized. She said she couldn't make it to the beauty parlor this week.

That's one way I know she's dying. And she was crying. She wasn't crying because she was glad to see me. She was glad, in her way. She misses me if she can't have a look at me every year or so.

I can remember my mother crying on only two occasions: when the dog died and when they found my brother dead. I remember both times vividly. With the dog it was a gentle, almost girlish sobbing, rather endearing. With my brother it was something else. She was like a gored beast.

My father was sitting at the dining-room table where he always sits. I was sitting where I always sit. He looked at me squarely in the eyes and said nothing. The look was a soft command: see what time and illness have done to me. See what's become of me, and what will become of you.

•   •   •

There's a moment of despair I experience returning to San Francisco after a visit east. It usually comes as the taxi is about to cross Haight Street, headed up the hill from the Panhandle. I'm not sure why it always hits me at that particular point. The ride in from the airport is sufficiently dreary to provoke such feelings as you head north along the western shore of the Bay with its billboards, warehouses, commercial buildings; then you make that turn and you're suddenly back in Oz.

It always seems to be early evening. Haight Street can be desolate, even repulsive, to be sure. But it's familiar to me after so many years, and I sometimes even like it, especially looking west to the park when the sky's doing something interesting. It all just feels so hopelessly nowhere at that particular moment, like this is really the end of the line. Like if you got on the 72 bus and took it another three miles west you'd fall off the earth. Then it passes, even as the cab heads up the hill to Frederick and turns right. Like a brief bout of nausea.

Mother and Father would come to visit, at least during my first few years out here. Father liked the idea of the place. As a boy he'd been mad for Jack London and that author's many youthful adventures here by the Bay. Mother hated it. Also, it upset her to be more than ten miles (or beyond toll-free telephone range) from her two sisters and Nanny Farbisseneh, who was now so old and so small that it was difficult to find her and ascertain whether or not she was still breathing. I can well remember Mother sitting in this very room, right on the couch over there, in fact, with her head in her hands, muttering, "I can't believe any human being actually lives like this."

I ran with a pack of cartoonists when I first arrived here. Mother didn't care for Petunia, my cartoonist girlfriend. We got through dinner at the Golden Dragon without incident, but when I saw Mother the next day she asked me if: (1) Petunia had had her "craniofacial deformity" since birth; and (2) if said deformity was the chief factor in her being a moron.

I never tire of the fog. It doesn't sit on the place; it moves through it, agitating the trees and other vegetation. If I look out the window, I can see bamboos and the tulip tree alive in it, likewise the morning glory that has climbed the palmetto, wrapping itself around as it went. Nor is it quiet: the wind carrying the fog in has a very distant, sustained roar, especially at night. It serves as a ground bass in the summer music of the place.

I find it consoling, like the rain. It is another layer between me and the world. The light is softer. Sounds are muffled. It pushes one inward, like the rain.

The day she left wasn't at all foggy. It was brilliantly clear and warm, as it often is here in late autumn. She was frightened, weeping—as well she might have been, still only a girl, really, going off to live in New York on her own.

I don't suppose she would have stayed, even if I'd asked her to. She had to go: she was long gone in her own head and we'd been miserable for months. I wanted her gone; I knew what it would do to me when she left.

It was difficult sitting there on the couch with her, waiting for the taxi to the airport that was taking forever. I went out into the backyard to get some air. The cat was chilling on the fence behind the peach tree and when he saw me sauntered along in my direction, arching his back and lifting his tail to be stroked. "Oh Christ, Patty," I remember saying, "this is going to be rough." He stared at me in that dispassionate, cross-eyed way of his, at once quizzical and mildly contemptuous. "You stupid sorry motherfucker," he seemed to be saying.

I don't know that the cat ever really got over the earthquake, the big one in '89. It's not as if Patty hadn't been through earthquakes before. I remember one time I saw him through the window, out in the backyard, with his head bobbing frantically while he went digging around the base of the peach tree for some roots to get hold of. But the '89 earthquake was something else. You don't soon forget one like that. I was at the back of the health-food store around the corner buying some arugula when the floor and shelves started trembling. Pretty soon the soba noodles and apricot-flavored whole wheat PowerBars were falling around my head and shoulders.

Most earthquakes seem to begin as if a big truck, an eighteen-wheeler carrying refrigerators or steel safes, is rumbling by just outside the door. Then everything quiets down after a few seconds. But if things don't quiet down and the shaking and rumbling keep on, that's when you run into some drama. Well, this one went on for about fifteen seconds, which doesn't seem like a long time unless you're in the middle of an earthquake. Time slows down and the shaking seems to double, triple, quadruple in force every few seconds, heading for a crescendo you know not how far down the road.

So there I am, trying to pay for my arugula and get the hell out of there before I'm conked on the head by an economy-sized bottle of Westbrae tamari sauce, when all of the shoppers in the place decide to migrate to the same doorframe at once, weeping and screaming and pushing each other out of the way because they have read that being in a doorframe is going to save them. I'm looking at some very poor behavior by twenty or so people in Birkenstocks.

Meanwhile, the clerk behind the counter is weeping uncontrollably and about to collapse, and the registers are down because there's no power. I make off with my arugula like the lowest sort of sneak thief and head back to the ranch, check out the damage, make a phone call or two, so forth. Well, there is no damage to speak of: a mirror fell over and cracked, a stack of Rubbermaid containers in the pantry collapsed and scattered. I got off easy. But there's the cat, on top of the mantelpiece in the living room, giving me this look like, "Now what have you gone and done?" I attempt to reason with him. That doesn't work. I try the tender-concerned routine. That doesn't work, either. I tickle him under the chin, behind the ear, beseech him to come down and enjoy a few Fishtabits. No dice. Patty's staying right where he is, and he's going to be staying there for the indeterminate future, no need for further discussion, none. I make like I'm going to pick him up when he gives me his ugliest tomcat look, as if to say, "Stay away from me you sick, crazy fuck."

Truth be told, I enjoyed the earthquake of '89; that is, until Dan Rather turned up with his camouflage costume and moue of concern. There was no power. The telephones weren't working. That first night the city was dark except for candles. It was a warm night, Indian summer. The whole city seemed to be out of doors. It was like an enormous block party, all the neighbors sitting on their stoops, drinking beer, listening to their radios.

San Francisco is an unfriendly city. Snooty. Cool, like its weather. The natty little old Slav three doors down could be a war criminal, for all I know. Once, his motor scooter, his pride and joy, tipped over and I helped him to pick it up. He nearly wept with gratitude but has never said hello or even acknowledged my existence, not before or since. But that night was different. People I'd seen around nearly every day for ten years who never uttered a single word or salutation were suddenly all over me like cheap carpets, introducing themselves, telling me where they were when the quake struck, asking if I'd lost anything. "My cat lost his mind, that's about it," I told them.

One set of neighbors decided, for reasons of their own, that my name was Dominic. Many new friendships were made that night. Many babies were born precisely nine months later. To this day all sorts of people in my neighborhood call me Dominic and, to a one, ask after my cat and want to know if he ever did come down from the mantelpiece.

Watching New York from the Palisades—well, that's the condition of living on the opposite shore: you watch. You watch the cars at night stream in and out of the city on the bridge and across the West Side Highway. The city trembles; it is a living thing, a kind of cell with nutrients and waste streaming in and out through its membrane, its vast mitochondria feeding deep inside of it, the whole thing throbbing with light.

New Jersey people who live along this stretch of the Hudson, directly across from the towers of Manhattan—I'm speaking here of the *Volk*, not the riffraff and carpetbaggers from somewhere else—believe they are getting the best of both worlds: the thrill and spectacle without the filth, expense, creeps, hustlers, and crap artists, which in the collective mind of New Jerseyites constitute the fabric of the great metropolis across the river.

New York is a thrilling city, not a pretty one, but from the Jersey side, Manhattan at night is among the most beautiful and dramatic spectacles on earth. Nothing I have ever seen in nature begins to match it, with the possible exception of the Grand Canyon.

Mother did not care for Melodia, either. Many who come to San Francisco from other parts of the country take on new, fantasy identities after arriving here. Melodia chose to be an English duchess, or what she imagined an English duchess to be like from assorted films and novels.

Melodia was very sophisticated. She was several years older than me and had been married and divorced at least twice. She retained the surname of one of her former husbands, a Québecois by the name of Gueule. This, presumably, made her Anglo-French, which is very high-class indeed.

Melodia spent all her money on Ferragamo shoes and made sensational pasta dishes, airy and complex. She was cultivated, too, and felt about J. S. Bach as Mother felt about Shakespeare. "Oh, the Partita no. 3 in A minor," she would shiver as it came on the radio, lightly drumming the lace fringe along the top of her bodice.

But what really drew me to Melodia, and encouraged my looking past her more outlandish affectations, was her taste for being tied up and sodomized, all the while muttering prayers in Latin that she had apparently been forced to commit to memory in the Midwest by the good sisters who presided over her parochial school education.

The meeting of Mother and Melodia, if inevitable, was not promising, or so it should have occurred to me. But Melodia and her shenanigans induced in me something akin to a sleep of reason, one that extended for the entire term of our relations.

It was at a Mexican restaurant, a swank affair at the foot of North Beach where you find many of the city's law and architectural concerns. Mother didn't like the restaurant. Mother didn't like San Francisco. Mother was in poor humor at the outset.

I had held out some small hope that Mother and Melodia might get along. After all, they were both of them big on couture and both insufferably vain. Melodia, for her part, was really decked out that evening, which is not to say that Mother's and Melodia's notions of "decked out" would have coincided: Melodia was given to plunging necklines, skirts with hems that rode perilously close to the curve of her delicious ass, ostentatious jewelry, this sort of thing. Melodia was, finally, an ignorant, trashy girl, which is why I adored her.

Around the time she stopped drinking scotch, Mother had decided that she was royalty. Her immediate antecedents, risen from a Ukrainian bog, seemed barely human to me, more like throwbacks to an earlier life-form, something amphibian but with the capacity for limited speech. Regardless, Mother now carried the mien of one to the manner born.

I suppose it was too much to hope that Melodia, with her English countess routine, and Mother, with her royal demeanor, would get along. There were problems. First, Melodia was stupid, and Mother was not. Which is not to say that Mother's intelligence could be characterized as far-ranging or inclusive, but the old girl did get it, I'll give her that. And one of the things she would have immediately got was that Melodia had designs on me, for marriage. You see, marriage for Melodia was what it must have been for Elizabeth Taylor and Barbara Hutton, no big thing; and in Melodia's case, a natural consequence of sodomy and prayer.

Mother sat between Melodia and me, with Father across the table, scowling at the prices on the dinner menu. I know what he was thinking: how can they get away with this markup when you're talking cornmeal and beans? Oblivious to it all, Melodia chattered away in her ditzy duchess way, saying nothing but filling the air with what she imagined to be the ambient noise of the British upper classes at play. Mother just sat there impassively with hooded eyes, coiled like a rattler. I should have been more alert, but thanks to the advice of the maître d', an unctuous, mustachioed character who could have passed for a croupier or high-level diplomat, I had made the acquaintance of an upmarket tequila, a golden ambrosial fluid, potent yet kind, and quite unlike the clear jet fuel to which I had been accustomed.

"Oh, Mrs. Klankensfelter, your son is the sweetest man in the world, and I simply have to tell you so, teeheeheee."

There was an extended, ominous pause, and from Mother's lips came the word "dear." Father's head snapped up from the menu. The curtains came abruptly down on my own little reverie. The word "dear," as Father and I knew only too well, coming out of Mother's mouth and directed at another female, meant that launch mode was locked in and under way. There would be no turning back. Father began waving spasmodically for the waiter, but he had disappeared long before, mistakenly believing, in his silly Latin way, that the four of us were there to enjoy a long, leisurely evening of dining and pleasant conversation.

"Dear," Mother repeated, turning slowly toward Melodia and fastening her with a gaze I've seen only once before, at the weigh-in before their first title fight in September 1962 when Sonny Liston turned toward poor, doomed Floyd Patterson and gave him that look.

"Dear," Mother repeated, a third and final time, "he's not sweet," nodding in my direction. "I'm not sweet," emphasizing that last word both by slowness of delivery and uncomfortably thorough elocution, then landing on the "t" with both heels. "And do you see that old man seated across the table?" pointing to Father and then looking at Melodia, who had taken on the aspect of a stunned mullet. "He's not sweet, either."

•   •   •

My father is poking me in the arm, the shoulder, provoca-
tively, and to the anxiety of the guests. They know of our
difficult relationship, probably of my father's unpredictable
and violent nature. But this is a game we have been playing
for nearly fifty years, alarming guests in this manner. He
shoves; I take it impassively, pretending it's not happening.
In fact, my father can barely contain his pleasure in seeing
me, that he has always taken in seeing me. Hitting me playfully in the arm is how he expresses his affection. Playing my
role is how I reciprocate this affection. "Do you see the way
that lunatic abuses the child and the child says nothing, pre-
tends it isn't even happening?" This was our shared joke on
the outside world.

He thinks I've come to the rescue, that I'm going to stick
around and look after them both. He's so grateful and relieved; he's been at his wit's end; now everything will be all
right. They're neither of them complainers, quite the opposite. They're freakishly dogged souls. They've got that old
Jersey City steel and stoicism running through them. I've
got a little of it myself, which has proved over the course of
my life to be both too much and not quite enough.

You go to the movies, put down your money, and get
to watch a tearful reconciliation between father and son,
mother and daughter, Paul and Yoko, whatever's going on
that particular Saturday night. But it doesn't play like that
back out in the world, on the sidewalk, opening your umbrella as you walk out from under the shelter of the marquee.

•   •   •

I'm staying at a hotel in the Village, the West Village, the same place I always stay. The years go by and the old Jamaican porter still recognizes me.

New York is shit above Fourteenth Street. I'd as soon be in St. Paul or Tulsa. One does, of course, need to go uptown for museums, dinner parties, the rest, but it's a trial, especially the Upper East Side. How do they stand it? The same way they stand East Bollocksville, I suppose.

She lives in the Village. Of course she does. Sensible girl. Not a girl anymore. A woman. Busiest woman in New York. The last time I saw her I felt like an astronaut going through one of those face-stretching, bone-rattling, g-force episodes. But it went okay. Ten years. A cup of tea. Okay. Now it's a breeze.

Strange not to experience that overpowering, almost sickening surge of desire anymore. Strange to be with her, chatting, having coffee outside that atmosphere. Makes her familiar and strange to me, being with her without all that. She's not easy to read. Never was. Wary, appraising, rather mysterious. How are the folks? Dying, actually. Oh . . .

"Have you ever loved anyone since as passionately as you loved me?" she asks.

Mother didn't quite know what to make of this one. She wouldn't have, would she? Of course, Melisande was very young, alarmingly so in relation to me. That alone would have fetched Mother's gimlet eye. But Melisande would have been a most unusual quantity for Mother, not least in her English parentage and upbringing. Mother knew from public television that being English and not of the servant class meant good breeding, perhaps even royal blood somewhere along the line. As royalty herself, Mother felt obliged to soften whatever disapproval she felt and, however reluctantly, to welcome young Melisande into her home.

Melisande herself, difficult to read and pleasantly demure in social situations like the one in which she found herself, where any sure footing would have been a dangerous illusion, for years afterward performed a cruelly accurate impersonation of Mother for all manner of dinner and party guests. Though my own relations with Mother were not the best, these performances were delivered with such relish and near perfect pitch that I confess now to having found them unsettling.

But what most forcefully claimed Mother's attention that warm October evening was my black eye. It was an inauspicious time to have a black eye, because the next day was the celebration of Mother and Father's fiftieth wedding anniversary. Mother took such occasions with the utmost seriousness, for they allowed her to exercise her full, and not inconsiderable, skills of generalship, skills she took great pride in and executed with imperious efficiency.

"What's with the shiner?"

I explained to Mother that that afternoon at a poetry reading in the city I went to the restroom and the prior occupant opened the door in my face.

"Poetry reading? Who do you think you're trying to kid?" Her contempt for the lamest, most pathetic bit of dissembling she had ever heard, ever, could not have been any less disguised. But what I told Mother was largely true. I had received my black eye at a poetry reading, but not exactly in the manner I described.

You see, Melisande was quite mad for poetry, at least in those days. Me, I'd rather be in a dentist's chair than go to one of those things where the lady poet whispers in her breathless little lady-poet voice about how come she's so out of sorts and Granny's moldering petticoat in the attic, this sort of drivel. But the poet-boy, he's worse still, striking this earnest pose—probably thinks it'll get him laid—and giving forth in these little spastic pellets about going fishing with the old man, getting things straight between them.

Well, that was one sort of poetry reading Melisande dragged me to, and that was wretched enough, but the one she took me to this particular Saturday afternoon at some gin mill way the hell downtown and west of Hudson Street, almost on the river, this one was something else. It seemed this dump had poetry readings on Saturday afternoons, "a long-running and distinguished series." The management turned off the ball game and the resident drunks all went to huddle in the far corner to make room for the poetry crowd, who, as far as I could tell, consisted exclusively of friends of the poet.

That afternoon the reader was an anorexic woman of indeterminate age wearing a crew cut. Her followers were a grim lot, with closely cropped hair and looking extremely concerned about the business at hand, as if attending a meeting of the IMF or the Atomic Energy Commission about to address a grave, perhaps ominous development on the Korean peninsula or Indian subcontinent.

With all of the affect of a dosed salamander, the poet picked up a thick sheaf of papers and announced, "I intend to read from my work in progress that many here will be fa-

4 0

miliar with [an appreciative hum in the audience] entitled 'Cnidaria.' For those of you who may be unfamiliar with my project, the long poem is entitled 'Cnidaria' because it is based on this particular phylum of aquatic invertebrates (better known as coelenterates) that includes hydra, jelly-fish, sea anemones, and corals. What specifically interests me about Cnidaria is its dioplastic body, with two cell layers of the body wall separated by mesoglea, which contain cells that have migrated from the two cell layers, but these cells do not form tissues or organs [more appreciative humming from the crowd, this last bit having touched a nerve among the gathered]. The body cavity is sac-shaped, with one open-ing acting as both mouth and anus [more appreciative hum-ming]. The subject of my poem is not the Cnidaria as a living, functioning organism per se. What I have done is to borrow its structure, not least its radial symmetry, for the structure of my poem, which has quite a different subject, if the term 'subject' is at all relevant here [more humming]. The subject of 'Cnidaria' is, finally, language [more appreciative hum-ming]."

"Melisande . . ."

"Shut up and pay attention."

I would not have understood what the poet was going on about even had she spoken slowly and in complete sen-tences. But she scrambled the syntax to such an extent as to make it incomprehensible and roared through her text at a rate designed to jam the signal of even the most ardent and devout among the semioticians and poststructuralists in the audience.

"Melisande . . ."

"Shut up."

I was most of the way through my fourth bourbon, rocks, when one of the house drunks, positioned sullenly in the corner, began his impersonation of the reader, quite a clever one I thought, something like a Bulgarian tractor manual read at seventy-eight rpm in a remorseless monotone. But Melisande was not amused, and, on realizing that her evil looks did nothing to shame or deter him, delivered a powerfully pneumatic "shhhhoosh." This only had the effect of provoking him further still, like pouring gasoline or, in this instance, alcohol on a fire. The gents were now beside themselves and the perturbation in the back of the bar was beginning to register among the poetry lovers at the front. Melisande's eyes narrowed. Though usually contained in public, like the proper English young woman she was, Melisande did have a temper, and it was now being brought to bear: "Hey, scumbag, button it!" This delivered in a very broad, unladylike Oxfordshire accent.

"Fuck you, bitch," came the response from the corner.

Well, you will understand my dilemma.

Father, unlike Mother, was thrilled with my black eye. An avid student and practitioner of the sweet science since boyhood, he wanted to see my knuckles in order to calculate what retribution I had brought down upon my antagonist(s). Father was thrilled with Melisande, and, after fixing her a large drink, dragged her into the living room to show off his latest crop of bodhisattvas.

All the next day, throughout their celebration—which must have seemed to Melisande as his first Kwakiutl potlatch seemed to Franz Boas—Father paraded Melisande and me among the guests, principally his male friends. It was as if, in middle age, I had finally done something right, something worthy of a good son: turned up on the old man's doorstep with a teenage girlfriend and a great big shiner.

The morning of September 11 I went off to shoot baskets over the hill. I certainly wasn't going to turn on the TV. I know what sort of obscenities America commits on itself with television during and after these things. It's a lovely walk to the courts. As lovely a walk in town as any I can imagine. I walk to the top of Stanyan, the last stretch absurdly steep for a residential street, and head up to Tank Hill.

San Francisco is beautiful. Whatever else it is or isn't, it is that. Especially from Tank Hill, where, on a clear day, as this one was, you can see a filmy blue band of the Pacific in the west, and then, tracking east, over Golden Gate Park and the Presidio, the Marin Headlands and Golden Gate Bridge, the Bay and the towers of downtown, the Bay Bridge, Oakland Hills, the Castro and Mission sprawling at your feet, and a fair way south along the Bay. It is a gift and a joy to live in such a place. And if the population is so narcissistically invested in this beauty as to be paralyzed by it, caught up in a stupor, I find the vantages no less stirring on account of it.

From Tank Hill I make my way down toward the courts along a network of hidden staircases between streets flanked by homes built close together on the sides of the steep hills, their gardens and the green public spaces the city looks after carefully planted with brodiaea, acanthus, lily of the Nile. On the narrower stairs, like the Saturn Steps, the vegetation presses in on you. You could be anywhere: Umbria, the south of France. The world goes on about its business and horror elsewhere.

Out on the streets, life went on as normal that morning: young mothers or Spanish nursemaids pushing strollers, trucks making deliveries. A group of Latino workmen clustered around a radio, taking in the extraordinary events. Then I was back in the world of the stairs, the purple flowers of the tibouchina, poppies, and valerian, the only sound that of birdsong.

The rains begin here around Halloween, the same time the clocks get put back an hour. All of a sudden it's dark. I always seem to be surprised and jarred by the abruptness of it. Overnight the place seems to shed its silliness, its pastel atmosphere of make-believe. It becomes not only a more real place but also a dark one: northern, more like Seattle or Vancouver than California. The darkness suits it. With the tourists long gone and countless hotel rooms empty, the place takes on its truer character: a windy, rain-lashed outpost on the edge of nowhere, just a big ol' frontier town with pretensions and fancified East Coast ways. It's the only time I feel rooted and at home here.

"Home Is Where You Come Across." This is the title of a song by the Houston-born singer and songwriter Chris Whitley, who has moved around a lot in his life and, at last word, lives near Berlin. It was a musician friend in New York who put me onto Whitley, a neighborhood friend from Jersey whom I've known for more than forty years. Kenny called me the other day on his cell phone, a filthy summer day in

New York, you know the kind: not a breath of air, ninety degrees, 90 percent humidity, truck exhaust, the elderly and infirm dropping like bowling pins.

"A Hungarian workman outside my building says to me, says, 'Sure is human out.' 'Sure is,' I tell him."

Here, on this end of the line, it was one of those summer days where the fogbank just sits offshore waiting for the signal to come in and the signal never arrives: clear blue skies, the air delicious, a hint of coolness in the sea breeze.

"I guess it's perfect out there, huh?" Kenny says.

"Yeah, as a matter of fact."

I find it so easy to talk with him. The inflections, the way sentences begin, suddenly stop or detour. There are all manner of unconscious codes embedded in this talk and I know them all, intimately, as I know my coffee mug or thumb. Huge blocks of information are conveyed in only a few words. Any more words would be not only unnecessary but a crudity, bad manners, an unwitting slight. Even words are bypassed at certain junctures, replaced by a pause or half-breathed silent laugh, the suspiration of assent. In person, words between us are barely necessary.

He is from the neighborhood, a place that no longer exists except in memory. Those of us from the neighborhood pass among others in this world, like the mendicants who carried with them the record of classical learning through the drear, cobbled passageways of the Dark Ages. Even if we don't remember one another or recognize the face, we are able to spot one another at crosswalks, shopping malls, train platforms. A look suffices. Nothing needs to be spoken.

•   •   •

I had promised myself. I had gone through it in my head well in advance, several times. I was simply not going to get into it. This would probably be our final few hours together. I was going to pull myself together. Restrain myself. Not go there. But there we were—there I was—having the same old political argument, in the same old way, across the dining-room table. Only the principals had changed. But I couldn't restrain myself. How could he be that irresponsible, that selfish, that obtuse . . . When I suddenly realized my father couldn't hear a goddamn word I was saying. He was stone-deaf. But there we were, locked into our old postures of confrontation, arms raised in the same gestures of exasperation and defiance, stylized as a couple of Kabuki actors performing a scene for the thousandth time. And there my mother was, what was left of her, in the kitchen doorway, expressionless, taking it all in—the three of us having somehow managed to find ourselves back in the same old tableau.

The morning's first streetcar comes out of the tunnel before dawn, about 5 a.m. It nearly passes under my backyard. Throughout the day into the late evening, passing in and out of the tunnel every twenty minutes or so, it punctuates, as well as announcing their beginning and end, my waking hours, with its rattling, squeals, and groans. This is my rough carillon.

I find it pleasant, reassuring, rather as I found living only a few blocks from the amusement park when I was a child. Over the course of the day, depending on the breeze, you could hear the muffled thunder of the celebrated "gravity-defying" rides: the Cyclone, Twister, Caterpillar, Whip. And in counterpoint, the shrieks of the patrons as they spun, plunged, and were turned upside down.

These sounds would continue well into the night, like the streetcar, and change in character over the course of the day, depending on the wind and weather. At night they would seem more distant, and sometimes disappear altogether for hours on end, only to return when you'd forgotten all about them. There was music, too: popular tunes broadcast over the loudspeakers. And at weekends, live talent, chart-busting new stars like Fabian, Little Anthony, Bobby Rydell.

One summer my older sister worked at the amusement park, and it was her job, every evening, to announce over the public address system that the fun was over and it was time for everybody to go home. I used to try to stay awake until I could hear my sister say good-bye to the customers, wish them well, and, at the conclusion, her voice distorted by the speaker system and barely audible through the night air: "Thank you, good night."

The rain was easing up a bit. It was late afternoon. My father was dozing off, my mother weeping fitfully.

"What's wrong, Ma?"

"Oh, nothing. I get the blues this time of day, is all. Normally, I'd have a drink around now, but I can't seem to be able to drink anymore for some reason. I don't know why."

It was time to go, let them have a rest. They'd had their look at me. There was nothing more I could do for them—take out the garbage, put the dishes in the dishwasher. Let them be. I phoned for a cab. There weren't any available. Maybe the weather. Who knows? I had to get out of there.

Borrow an umbrella and walk to the bridge. It was only a couple of miles, not even. I'd done it a thousand times.

My mother walked in. "I'll take you," she said. I protested chivalrously. Don't trouble yourself. I'll steal an umbrella. You must have an extra one knocking around. But she was keen to drive me to the ferry. Said she had to get out of the house or she'd go crazy. Sitting in her driver's seat was the only time her back didn't hurt.

I wanted to oblige her. She was so miserable and in such discomfort. But she was horribly frail; I don't know how she managed to keep herself upright. And then there was the weeping. I was frightened about getting into a car with her behind the wheel. "Don't be frightened," she said, reading my mind. "I can drive."

And she could, much to my surprise. With my father slumped in the backseat, very quiet, we drove the five or six miles to the Weehawken ferry with no problems. Sunday, late afternoon, not much traffic.

The rain had begun falling lightly again as we pulled into the drop-off area. I could smell the river. You could barely make out the city across the way, its grays and charcoals having blended into the mist, like one of Monet's blurry Paris cityscapes.

"It was good to see you, Ma."

"Oh, it really was terrific seeing you, Augie," she said. "It was a thrill for me, it really was." And she meant it. I could tell she did. She had no need or particular desire to see me again in this life, but it did seem to nourish her, having me around to look at for a couple of hours.

I kissed her on the cheek and turned to say good-bye to my father. He was huddled in the corner of the backseat looking glum and rather cold. He couldn't seem to keep warm, no matter how high the heating was turned up or how much clothing he put on. I'm not sure what was going through his head. I tried my best to lean over the back of the seat and kiss him good-bye, but it was awkward. I couldn't reach very far. He leaned toward me halfheartedly. I suppose I could have gotten out, opened the back door, and given him a proper kiss and hug, but he wasn't looking as if it would have made his day. I squeezed his hand gently and told him it had been good to see him.

And that's when it came out of me, in this half-strangled sob (I still cringe to think of it): "I'll try to be a better son." But it didn't matter. He wouldn't have heard me anyway.

Part Two

THE LOST EVENING

Since it was Christmas Eve, I thought it might be the appropriate time to go see a movie about a writer who endeavors to drink himself to death. I phoned my friend Windrow, who makes furniture in the lower Haight, and invited him along. Windrow has been known to enjoy a drink now and then, and he's also a renowned noir novelist—in France, that is. Here he's a furniture maker, there he's a cult novelist. Sloe-eyed North African dollies stalk him and write him mash notes, drunk French belletrists try to pick fights with him—his other life across the sea. I have no thoughts about the former, but the latter bewilders me: (1) Windrow is a big ol' boy from North Carolina who makes his living with his hands; and (2) he is the most gregarious and least combative of souls, quite opposite to most of the characters who roam the hard-boiled pages of his novels for the Rivages/Noir house, with titles like *Les Damnés ne meurent jamais*, *Le Démon dans ma tête*, *Injection mortelle*, this sort of thing.

Windrow liked the idea and needed no arm-twisting. The plan was to walk across town to the Lumière and see what the streets were like. We had a couple of pops of holiday cheer at his apartment above the shop to get us in the mood and presently were on our way. It was a fine afternoon, cool and sunny. The 49ers had just lost a nasty little affair to Atlanta. Not too many folks on Market, the usual mix: homeless with shopping carts; people in costume; a couple of kids, maybe from Salinas, looking for something or other and not succeeding in finding it. I'm told Market was a grand street once, before the Second World War. That's tough to believe, especially the stretch from Laguna to Taylor, which nowadays feels more like Heartbreak Corridor. In any case, Windrow and I found ourselves running late so had to jump on a 42 bus. Windrow confessed that he hadn't been on a bus in several years and was excited, it seemed. The young woman sitting in front of us looked nervous, possibly made so by Windrow's volubility. One guesses sometimes at what's going through the minds of people on public conveyances by the expressions on their faces. And one guesses nearly always wrong.

When the soundtrack is as loud and slick and rotten as it is on *Leaving Las Vegas* you know you're in for a long two hours. Jane Campion's *The Piano* was like that. When you were hit with that New Age Muzak at its beginning you knew the director had no taste. *The Piano* was an insufferably arty, ponderous, and pretentious film, but it wouldn't have been quite so unendurable if Liszt, say, were being played on the piano instead of Michael Nyman. Mike Figgis, who directed *Leaving Las Vegas*, is responsible for the soundtrack, on which he also plays trumpet. I believe he had a hand in the script as well. In fact, it could only have been Figgis. The soundtrack consists for the most part of someone called Sting butchering old torch songs, beautiful songs like "My One and Only Love." (Listen to Johnny Hartman sing it with Coltrane behind him sometime.) There is, however, during one among countless anguished moments in the film, a noise that I can describe only as a Tyrolean yodeler in the midst of a colonoscopy. That was very good, and there was another moment when the protagonists were outside of Vegas at a desert hotel and a coyote comes in hard on the heels of one of Sting's gold lamé interpretations, much as a hound bays in the wake of police and fire sirens. That was good as well.

Here's the setup: A Hollywood writer (?), Nicolas Cage, has an industrial-strength drinking problem and talks very loudly in airports and bars about women's genitalia and how he would like to pour liquor on these genitalia and so on, making an enormous nuisance of himself. His boss at the movie studio evidently finds out about this and decides to let him go, whereupon Cage packs his belongings into fifteen garbage bags and leaves them out front of his L.A. stucco bungalow for the garbagemen and heads off into the desert with thirty bottles of hooch. There's a nice shot of the mountains.

The silliest aspect of this intensely silly movie is the drinking. The Cage character goes through bottles of vodka, tequila, bourbon like a 285-pound offensive lineman from Florida State drinking Gatorade. I enjoy bars, and San Francisco has quite a few good ones, and I've had ringside seats more than once at the spectacle of someone destroying himself with alcohol. I have no idea what Figgis has Cage doing. By my estimate his character is consuming about three gallons of hard liquor per day before he turns to beer and then back to tequila, stingers, screwdrivers, Bloody Marys. He does allude to vomiting at one point and, in fact, does retch rather daintily into a basin near the end of the movie. But otherwise, though he slurs his speech and lists to port or starboard now and then, he manages to drive, be almost witty, inquire after women's genitalia, and generally take care of business, or not take care of business, as it were. The heroic bout of drinking that allegedly finished off Dylan Thomas at the White Horse Tavern wouldn't have even gotten our Hollywood writer friend past the morning shakes.

But no matter, back to the plot. Upon arriving in Las Vegas and booking into The Whole Year Inn, which is transformed by his blitzkrieged vision into The Hole You're In, he drinks several gallons of scotch, vodka, and tequila and decides to have a leisurely drive around town. At a stoplight he runs into a pretty young hooker played by Elisabeth Shue and inquires of her genitalia. They drive back to his place and it turns out after all those inquiries about private parts that what he really wants to do is cuddle. The Shue character falls in love with him straightaway—no doubt cuddling sounds pretty good after the day she's already had. She invites him to move in with her. Most of the dialogue from this point on consists of Shue asking Cage, "Are you all right?" (No, silly, he's not all right; he's pissed as a newt.)

The leitmotif amid the vicissitudes of a drunk and a hooker in Las Vegas is the gorgeous Ms. Shue's attempts to get Cage to screw her. Surely every male in the audience (and Windrow and I were the oldest) was crying out to the Cage character in his heart, "Pull yourself together, schmuck, and give it the old college try!" But it is not until the very end of the movie (I hope I'm not giving too much away here) that their union is consummated. The divine Ms. Shue mounts the quivering, moribund Cage (who at this point would be bleeding from the mouth and anus, not to mention suffering from Korsakoff's psychosis and polyneuropathy) and a gentle copulation transpires. How he managed an erection at this stage eludes me, but to quote from a naughty old blues, Ms. Shue's character "could make a dead man come." Which Mr. Cage does and promptly drops dead.

'Tis a consummation devoutly to be wished, but I felt bad for Nicolas Cage nonetheless. He has a long, hangdog clown face, deadpan funny, and is a likable presence on screen. When he smiles he can look the kind of handsome that I'd imagine makes him endearing and attractive to women. It's an impossible part to bring off, but he can't act, regardless. Neither can I, for that matter. It's no big thing. He tries terribly hard and does a god-awful lot of shaking and the overwrought routine until the cumulative effect is like a very, very long skit from *Saturday Night Live*. I blame this and everything else wrong with the movie on Mike Figgis, the director. I was later told that the film was based on a novel by John O'Brien, who killed himself, probably after seeing what Figgis did to his book. But I cannot vouch for the teller of that tale, nor would I.

The cinematography is boilerplate for these days, with the standard fades and what Windrow likes to call "candy-apple reds," by which he means color saturation and lots of primary colors, which he tells me come out of the old *Miami Vice* TV series. Windrow doesn't have a TV so somebody probably told him this. My TV is black-and-white, and all I recall of *Miami Vice* are two cops, one black, one white, who seemed to get rid of the pretty women as quickly as possible so that they could be alone together and admire one another's threads and buttocks. Ah, yes, and a melodramatic synthesizer soundtrack.

Elisabeth Shue, however, is not only a beautiful young woman but also a fine actress. She can't carry the movie—a C-140 transport couldn't do that—but she's the reason I didn't walk out, not that Windrow would have let me, and he had the aisle seat. Her character unaccountably changes early in the film from being a helpless ditz to an emotionally complex young woman. One would like to believe she is transformed by her love for the Cage character, but it's merely one of the countless holes in the script. She has no real lines, no director, no leading man, and she still manages to be riveting. That's something special. American actresses are seldom attractive. They're not really supposed to be, just as Americans are not really supposed to enjoy sex or food. Elisabeth Shue is. There's also a very fine cameo by an older actress whose name I'm afraid I missed in the credits. She plays the manager of the little motel the two principals go to in order to chill out and attempt romance. During yet another of Shue's desperate, and delicious, attempts to get Cage into bed, the drunken Cage character demolishes a glass table. The manager cleans up the mess and very sweetly, very icily tells Ms. Shue to take her "loud-talking ways" back to their room and be out in the morning. It's the best performance in the movie and no more than a minute long, certainly no reason to fork over seven and a half bucks.

I don't know what Polk Gulch was like in Frank Norris's time, but in a town filled with good bars it's slim pickings these days around California and Polk. There was a sad little dive a couple of doors down from the theater, though, and

Windrow and I were in sore need of refreshment after the ordeal of Nicolas Cage's ordeal. We found a couple of stools next to the Foosball table and I asked Windrow what he thought of the film. "I liked it," he said, much to my surprise. It wasn't easy to hear in the place; they had the Ramones cranked to a decibel level that only old Led Zeppelin fans could endure. But this is what Windrow said: He liked the setup, two desperate characters at the ends of their tethers linking up. That's the kind of subject he liked to write about himself. He adored Ms. Shue. He was willing to look past the ludicrous drinking, the bizarrely incongruous Lithuanian pimp (I left him out), the want of a script, and so forth. Windrow said one should think of the film not in the context of drunk movies like *Lost Weekend* and *Days of Wine and Roses*, but as kindred to *La Grande Bouffe*. It's about hyperbole, he was saying, when we were interrupted by a young woman who had been shooting pool nearby. She was petite, all cheekbones and red lipstick, pancake makeup, and a black Henry VIII hat over hair dyed a kind of white I'd seen on young women before but that didn't look too healthy in the bar light. She was very eager to chat, which led me to believe she was either a transvestite or a hooker. Windrow and I had another round, just to find out. She called herself Gigi and had these peculiarly aggressive conversational gambits, such as, "If you were on a desert island with your best friend and he had cancer and a hundred thousand dollars . . ." What emerged after some time was that she had decided that we were *managers* and she wanted business advice. She took her hat off and turned it inside out. It was reversible, crimson. Then she turned it into a handbag. Amazing. She made these

things and wanted to know what we thought was a reasonable markup. Windrow was most helpful and forthcoming in
this regard and Gigi was clearly warming up. But Windrow is
happily married, and I have arrived at that age and station
in life where it ill behooves me to tarry with young strangers,
so we bade the enterprising Gigi adieu and headed into the
night.

THE BUS

One of the inadvertent pleasures of life is getting stuck. We, some of us, understand, as regards travel, that much of the pleasure is in the getting there, and being waylaid somewhere one might not ordinarily have chosen to visit for any length of time can turn out to be an interesting, even instructive, adventure. But we Americans are not too ready to buy into that possibility, choosing instead to demolish mountainsides, tunnel under rivers, and lay hundreds of miles of asphalt over the most productive soil on earth simply to expedite arrival at our destination, even if bad news awaits us there. It is the American way, dammit.

But one still gets *stuck* here in America now and then, in spite of ourselves. And here I am in downtown San Diego waiting for the number 7 bus, and waiting and waiting, because I am on assignment to write a magazine piece about the exotic experience of riding a municipal bus in a city where 98 percent of the population would never even consider such a method of transportation. Thus, I find myself on one of Broadway's seamier corners, a patch of ground I would not have chosen to spend an hour of my time, and discover, as one who makes himself available to accidents of this sort often does, that it is as commendable a place as any for inspecting several square yards of sidewalk and all that clusters atop and beside it, as well as what passes it by.

For instance, when I turn away from the street, a 180 degree-er, and a neat job of it, too, I find myself face-to-face —separated by plate glass, that is—with two wonderfully attractive young women, side by side, one very black, one very white, clearly friends, seated on stools, eating fried chicken and staring back with a certain beguiling audacity at the balding, middle-aged man with his notepad and pen staring back at them. I look up: LOUISIANA FRIED CHICKEN. I look back down at the ladies. They look at me.

I love to watch a good-looking young woman eat. Forgive me. It is, I think, not so much a salacious thing as an aesthetic one. It is, quite simply, one of the spectacles in this life that I hold dearest to my heart. I did not wonder if the batter was peppery or crisp, or if the meat was tender. I didn't speculate on whether their undergarments that day were sensible or naughty. I was transported by the way they worked over their respective drumsticks. Now, quite reasonably, they looked back at me like I was your garden-variety doofus and, though I couldn't make out the precise content, I surmised by their giggles and looks of contempt that their conversation between bites somehow involved me and my general character, and probably not in an altogether flattering context.

The poet Ezra Pound once wrote that the life of a village is narrative and the life of a city cinematic. Which strikes me as true in many regards, and certainly the view of a city through the window of a car or bus is cinematic, though with Mr. de Kooning around 1960 or so, it becomes something else, equally dynamic, in paint. Be that as it may, waiting for a bus to show up while occupying a patch along a busy stretch of pavement feels slower to me than film, more along the lines of reading: a block like a sentence, a neighborhood like a paragraph, and so on. Of course, this depends on how busy that stretch of pavement is; things can turn cinematic in a hurry, if you follow me. But if it's not too frantic and you're stuck there for quite some time, reading and rereading those same few sentences, after a while you get a feeling for the texture of it all: the nouns and verbs, the movement; the syntax of the place begins to sink in.

Broadway and Fifth, noonish, on a weekday, ain't the Champs-Élysées, to be sure, but it has a distinctive life of its own, defined as much by what or who it hasn't got as by what it does. You can buy a pair of Payless shoes and have them repaired three shops over. You can go eat some fried chicken with the girls and then, next door, enjoy a doughnut for dessert. Then, if you're of a mind, you can go get your ears pierced and your beads strung at the jewelry store.

An older woman, looking a bit rough from the vicissitudes of this life, perhaps in tandem with a taste for the lower end of the vintner's art, saw me standing there in my sports coat with pad and pen, taking notes in front of the jewelry shop's display window. She approached me and remarked, with some conviction, "They're displaying them wrong." "What?" I inquired. "Them watches there, see?" "What's the matter with them?" "They're sideways, see? They oughta be frontways so you can have a real look." Her logic was not entirely lost on me. "Why don't you go inside and tell them?" I asked. "That's *your* job," she responded in no uncertain terms, eyeballing the jacket and notepad. And perhaps she was right. She was almost certainly right, but the number 7 bus just then swept up to the curb in all of its rectangular majesty.

I've ridden a fair number of buses in my day. I even have a license in British Columbia (doubtless lapsed) to drive a school bus. You get one of those along with your taxi license for some reason. Why, only a fortnight before I'd been on one of those London double-decker buses, which turned out to be an uncomfortable, spartan affair, not at all as one might have imagined with Petula Clark crooning away in the driver's seat. I've ridden buses from Hackensack to Auckland: minibuses, diesel buses, trolley buses, touring buses with tinted glass, Greyhounds across the Canadian prairies and from New York to Montreal, the latter stuffed with Hasidim and Haitians. I've ridden hippie buses up and down the West Coast. I've been pushed around by British soldiers on a Belfast bus when I wandered too far from my rucksack. I've slept on buses and awakened I know not where on buses. I routinely get lost on buses. I can tell you the pros and cons of bus terminals from Port Angeles to Sault Sainte Marie. I've read a good, ugly little novel by Denis Johnson about an amorous connection on a bus that goes terribly wrong. My memory is not what it once was, but I don't recall making any amorous connections on buses. Though I can say for certain that I've ridden on buses with a sweetheart or two. Though not lately. Even sweethearts, these days, tend to have their own cars.

As it turns out, there were two sweethearts on this very bus, the number 7, and they had been standing on the very same corner nearly as long as I, holding hands. If you were casting for *Romeo and Juliet*, these two gentle pilgrims would not have jumped out of the line at you. They had both seen better days, and they had had quite a few less good days under their belts since then. Please don't think me harsh or judgmental. I myself resemble a dissipated accountant who worked some years as a hod carrier in his youth. These two lovers were in their forties, I should guess, their faces worn well beyond that. By drink, probably, hard times, too many nights out of doors. They looked as many of the homeless look where I live, in San Francisco.

But there they were, filled with tenderness for each other, clearly no need to speak, her weathered head on the shoulder of his very un-dry-cleaned jacket. I tried not to stare, and they were too beat-up and tuned in to one another to care, but I was touched by them and by how feeling of that kind managed to flourish in such meager soil.

The bus was an articulated affair, relatively new, the seats in the rear made of molded plastic and less comfortable than the upholstered seats in the forepart of the vehicle. I wouldn't say the two sets of seats were optimally coordinated with regard to color and design, but that's not one of my areas of expertise; they seemed tolerable-looking enough so far as I was concerned, and my concern was the articulated part of the bus, the part where it's rubber on the outside and one can swivel around a bit on the turns. That's where I like to sit. Quite the thrill it is, too. But then, I figured, what with the sports jacket and notepad, I'd be calling attention to myself, so I decided to take a seat at the back, try to appear nondescript. There was no need for anyone to know I was a well-seasoned professional in getting around town on public transport.

You see, I don't own a car. Oh, I can drive just fine, but I take no pleasure in driving and, in truth, can't really afford a car, at least not in San Francisco, where there is little need for one. I have friends who get into their cars like they're walking into a party or a pretty gal's bedroom. Just as soon drive all day. Spend hours under the hoods of their cars making discoveries of all sorts. I had a friend once come down from Alaska and spend the whole winter here at my place in San Francisco. He had brought his old Volvo with him down from Juneau on the boat. My friend spent the whole four months under that car, all day, every day, and came in every evening dirty, satisfied, and filled with revelations about the mechanical universe. I once had a car, for six months. Bought it from an ex-girlfriend when she left town. Stupidest goddamn thing I've ever done. Sold it to some poor sucker for $600, what I paid for it.

The *"PASAJES—Favor de pager el pasaje exacto, Normal"* is $1.75 here in San Diego. In San Francisco it is $1.25 and in NYC $1.50. Mind you, I was not on the bus to La Jolla or Coronado or Torrey Pines, but I can assure you that the passengers aboard the number 7 looked as if they understood the full value of $1.75. My *pasaje* is being taken care of by a local paper, which has commissioned an article about taking the number 7 bus to El Cajon, the end of the line. There is nothing of interest in El Cajon. Frank Zappa and Captain Beefheart strummed a few chords in El Cajon while growing up. Ted Williams hit a home run in El Cajon, maybe, while in high school. El Cajon is the end of the line.

Apart from the extravagant fare, I noticed that there was

next to no advertising. I consider myself an aficionado of public transit overhead advertising. I should qualify my appreciation of the medium by explaining that it was acquired passively, often while being squashed against an aluminum handrail, with someone's shoulder under my neck and another's backpack pushing behind it, so in that posture, head upraised, I might be seen as taking absolution, when in reality I am gazing into the dark eyes and clear complexion of a handsome Puerto Ricana of a certain age with the following underneath:

ZUCKERMAN, SCHMALP,
ALVAREZ & JACKSON, MDs
Trained and Expert Dermatologists
REMOVE
LASER, ELECTROLYSIS,
RADIATION, PENKNIFE
pimples, chancres, buboes
warts, moles, wens, boils, blackheads, crow's feet
laugh lines, frown lines, bags
goiters, cysts
humps
AND UNWANTED HAIR
Reasonable rates, payment plan
CALL NOW
1-800-CUT-UGLY

You don't run across too many Lexus ads or give-that-special-someone-a-diamond ads on the bus or subway. There's a reason for that. But I have always been taken by the genre of overhead advertising to be found on public transport: the ads for sore feet, piles, fast loans, marriage counseling, community college courses, March of Dimes . . .

The number 7 bus was out of downtown, or what passes for downtown in San Diego, by the 900 block of Broadway. I began to spot some ample, ugly residential apartment buildings. We passed a crummy-looking dive called the Hong Kong Nile Club. Simply the name of the place made my assignment worthwhile, and the look of it as well, at least from the street: its front door open, someone, maybe the owner or bartender, having a smoke outside. One couldn't see into the shadows (one of the secret pleasures of daytime drinking). I certainly harbored no urge to jump off the bus and go in for a beer. Maybe they even had a tired stripper going through the motions on a makeshift stage, if the local laws allowed. I've been in a hundred scuzzy joints like that in a hundred downtowns. They're all pretty much the same. The fancier ones have younger girls, sometimes two or three, and several TVs going, each with a different game. When I was younger these places had a certain allure for me. Now it's merely the name—Hong Kong Nile Club—that gets me going. I decide then and there that'll be the title of my next book.*

Not much farther along we passed a motel called the Parkside Inn that also got me going. What's that line—is it in the Emmylou Harris song?—"cut-rate romance, low-rent rendezvous." I'm sure its rooms are clean and well-appointed,

*Only later would I discover that the neon on the crossbar of the "t" had burned out and that it was the Hong Kong Nite Club, which would have interested me not at all.

the staff friendly, and the clientele of the very first stripe, but it struck me as hardly the place to take a lady of good breeding, even for an afternoon of Chinese checkers and polite conversation, unless, perhaps, you ran across her in the Hong Kong Nile Club.

Southern California exists for me primarily as an abstraction, a composite of movies and the noir fiction of Raymond Chandler, Ross Macdonald, and James M. Cain. My visits to the region have been few and far between, but I see Mildred Pierce in every woman at the local Vons. Weakness and treachery lie barely concealed in almost every face. I am possessed by Philip Marlowe and Lew Archer. My view of mankind dims. Everyone's got a secret. Everyone's got an angle.

It would take some imagination to credit the passengers aboard the number 7 with much in the way of angles, at least any by which they may have achieved undue advantage. Quite the opposite, I should have guessed. Easterners like myself, even after more than twenty years out West, carry around a prejudice with them about Californians, particularly Southern Californians. Even San Franciscans, and Northern Californians in general, hold a similar prejudice: that the south of the state is a catch basin for all the losers and scoundrels of the continent, which, somehow, tilts south and west, leaving all the high-minded types in Boston, New York, and Washington, D.C., and, of course, San Francisco.

No, the passengers aboard the number 7, in a wealthy city that likes to vote Republican, were the detritus, the servants, the newly arrived, a few of the women—short, squarely built, ancient-looking faces—like Mayan or Guatemalan carvings I saw as a child in the museum: tired, wary faces, not at all like Joan Crawford trying to put one over on Jack Carson and the others. I suspect some food and rest was the angle with most of them on the number 7.

I enjoy watching people. I think I get that from my mother. I enjoy being anonymous, which I probably get from my father. That's why cities suit me. *Flânerie*, that's my thing. I find it absolutely paralyzing to spend any time in a small town. Everybody knows, or thinks they know, you, what you've got going on in your life. They know what you buy and how much you usually spend at the food store, the liquor store, the dry goods store. Extrapolate from there and it really starts getting a bit close.

The view picks up once we cross over the freeway and into the magnificently commodious Balboa Park, stopping at the naval hospital. You could see the Coronado Bay Bridge in the distance, and the park's greenery, along with the little bit of elevation, was refreshing after that long stretch of Eleventh Avenue. The bus was perhaps two-thirds full, the passengers a mix of races. By Marlborough Avenue farther along the route, down University Avenue, the bus would be almost all Hispanic. A couple of blacks. For most of the route I was the only white.

A young couple, very young, got on the bus and sat nearby. They had a small son. The mother was attractive, a Latina, with intelligence in her eyes. The child was sweet. Papa scratched his nuts and picked his nose. The little boy drifted off to sleep with his head on his mother's breast and then woke up after a short while. The mother passed along the child to the father. The child, still half asleep, opened his eyes and, when it was his father he saw, emitted an intensely happy gurgle and hum that seemed to issue from the very middle of him. The young father seemed most pleased with his son and set him down across his fat belly, where the child once again fell asleep.

We were climbing, not much of a grade but steadily uphill. Kung fu parlors. Speed 99¢. A whole selection of 99¢ shops. Tire shops. Fast food. Furniture: "financing and layaway available." Nails. Beauty. Car washes. Kitty Kat Adult Theater. A large new stretch of highway construction intersecting University. More Asian businesses by the time you reach Highland. Desolate-looking residential streets fanning out from the avenue. Who lives in these places? Video rentals. Optometrists. Taquerías. All of life's essentials . . .

The "all-purpose, intense, high-speed linear corridor": this post–World War II phenomenon is documented in an excellent book by Chester H. Liebs called *Main Street to Miracle Mile*. As revolting as you or I may find it, Liebs is not at all dismissive of the phenomenon; in fact, he finds all sorts of architectural novelties and gems among what may seem an incoherent mess: entrepreneurial appetite gone unchecked along with planning restraints and zoning laws. University Avenue is pretty dreadful, but a wee bit less so after reading Liebs, at least in the sense that knowledge, to some extent, neutralizes fear and loathing: "architecture for speed reading," Liebs calls it, "The Movie Through the Windshield."

Streaming out from the central city, through fringetown and all across the country, a gaudy honky-tonk slowly filled up the great American road. At first it was limited to wayside gas stations and restaurants needed by the traveler. But then came his lodging shops and entertainment to capture him. Market St., Front St., Times Square and Coney Island all exploded into the country and took root on a broader scale than ever possible in the city. The new motorized fairyland offered something for everyone: frozen custards, pizza pies and foot-long hot dogs; golf, baseball, shooting ranges; wild animals, snake pits, frontier villages; Kozy Kabins and lush Hollywood Motels; drive-in movies, drive-in banks, drive-in churches; steak palaces, gin mills, burly shows. Bigger merchants, too, saw the scale of the new moving market and came out to flag it down. The scale of disorder grew with supermarkets, used-car lots, seat-cover showrooms, outdoor furniture stores, do-it-yourself centers, discount houses, pipe-rack clothing chains.

> ("Roadtown: The Great American Excursion,"
> *Architectural Forum* 105 [September 1956]: 124)

Yeah, well . . . Read as a book or viewed as a movie, this patch of hell—the ten or so miles of University Avenue that the number 7 runs along—is beginning to bring on the soul sickness that I suffer from time to time in places like Toronto and Minneapolis, those Protestant fortresses of boosterism and commerce. Once I nearly had a full-fledged nervous collapse at a Denny's in Bemidji, Minnesota, my heart breaking into a thousand pieces while I chewed a wooden-tasting BLT. I never know where it will afflict me; perhaps it has to do with biorhythms. No, check that: I know it's not going to afflict me in Bologna's Piazza Maggiore or while dining in the Marais.

There sure are a lot of acupressure joints along this strip, and the occasional palm tree and all the terra-cotta tiles tell you you're not in Hartford, on your way to the airport. The best building on view along the entire strip, for my money, is a little tower at University and Forty-seventh, part wedding cake, part Walt Disney, part Leaning Tower of Hidey-Ho Heights, called, suitably enough, The Tower. It is a bar, with a Wienerschnitzel franchise close by for when your appetite kicks in. That little patch had my name on it, and I make note for the way back, lest I be needing fortification to get me through my soul sickness.

But the thing that distinguishes University Avenue from a thousand other hell corridors just like it is the topography around it and through which it's cut; that is, what's left of it. By its look, the bulldozers and demolition boys were left to make it up as they went along. And those elevated bits on either side of the highway, especially on the south side, are probably old beach ridges consisting of sediment laid down during a lowering of sea level 2.5 million years ago. What the bulldozers were leveling off for housing was old beach and dune.

The town of La Mesa must be pushing sixty thousand citizens these days. It was incorporated in 1912. There was one homicide in 1995, three in 1994, one in 1993, two in 1992, another two in 1991, only one in 1990, and none whatsoever in 1989. Its biggest annual event is Oktoberfest, during which the Wienerschnitzel folks from down the road presumably turn up in force. *The City & Town Profile* book about San Diego in the library says of the place: "A nice-looking city in a suburban way. Residents mow the lawns, trim shrubs, apply the paint brush ... Served by buses and trolleys. Two freeways and a parkway. Not the best of commutes in San Diego County but far from the worst." It might have gone on to add that if the pod people from the *Invasion of the Body Snatchers* passed through town, it would be pretty dang difficult to tell who got turned and who stayed the same.

It was chilly when I got off the bus in "downtown La Mesa." We really had, it seemed, put a little altitude under us. There was the La Mesa Library and the Foothills Fine Arts Gallery, the post office and police station. Behind the town to the east was a nice hill with trees on either side of its ridge that made it look like a bear's head. Suddenly, I was hungry. I hadn't eaten lunch. I remembered that a couple of hundred yards back we'd driven by a mall, the La Mesa Spring Mall, and headed in that direction. There were no sidewalks; in Southern California, when on foot, one goes parking lot to parking lot, if one goes at all, while everyone stares at you with a combination of bewilderment and suspicion from their car windows.

It was going to be slim pickin's—I understood this before I had a look around. I went into a Round Table Pizza. It was late for lunch, past two. No one around. A cartoon show going noisily on the big-screen TV. There was some food under a heat lamp that looked like pizza. "One dollar," the chief authority in the establishment muttered without enthusiasm. I took a piece without meat on it. I figured tired meat can hurt you worse than tired vegetables. It wasn't much of a slice, even for only a buck. I decided to have dessert.

I discovered a Panda Express a couple of doors down. It wasn't nearly as gloomy or empty as the Round Table, but the fare in the steam trays didn't look any more inviting. A dish called "teriyaki chicken" looked as if it should have been called "red-dye #2 chicken." There was something called pepper chicken that looked harmless enough. "For sixty cents you get another entrée," the young Chinese man behind the counter volunteered, smiling an alarming pod-person smile that he was probably fitted for at the Panda Academy, or maybe he'd spent a couple of weekends at the Panda Motivational Institute.

I saw in a tray a pile of beef and broccoli. The beef was coated with a brown, cornstarch-like film that made it look like a waste product of extraterrestrials. The alien motif was beginning to kick in with a vengeance at this point, perhaps fueled by hunger and light-headedness from the altitude. But I coveted some broccoli right then and said, "Just give me some broccoli, if you please." The kid gave me quite a pile of broccoli, probably relieved to be rid of it, and I went to my little plastic table and chair with a large pile of dismal-looking tucker.

At that point, the afternoon perked up. Two young black women at the table next to me started hollering, "Hey, that's no fair, you told us you gotta take it like it comes, not special like more broccoli for that guy!" Discerning immediately that these girls, unlike the pod people serving us, had not been as yet taken over by aliens, I offered them a share of my broccoli, not to mention my pepper chicken, but they were not so much interested in my plate as in an earlier beef-and-broccoli exchange. It seemed that the young ladies had asked the chap behind the counter for only beef, no broccoli. As a graduate of the Panda Express Institute of Higher Learning, he knew that beef was more expensive than broccoli and told the young ladies that there would be no customized orders at the Panda Express, not now, not ever, company policy.

So you might imagine their pique when I was afforded a customized order. The young ladies began carrying on in earnest, but the manager held firm, waving them off with a haughty gesture from behind the counter. Bad strategy. This displeased the young ladies, and they took a new tack. One of them worked in an office, she announced, that had a certain affiliation with (or at least the phone number of) the Better Business Bureau. This caught the manager's attention. The ladies warmed up to their new tack. Not only were they going to the Better Business Bureau about the beef-and-broccoli matter, they decided they had been "unfairly discriminated against on the basis of color." Whoa, Katie bar the door! *This* got the young manager's attention big-time. *DENNY'S DENNY'S DENNY'S* went off like a car alarm in his head, the restaurant chain having been pressured only recently into a large cash settlement over a similar complaint. I am no longer in Mr. Liebs's movie, blessedly, at least for the time being. And I find myself exiting Don Siegel's *Invasion of the Body Snatchers*, filmed in 1956 in a fictitious Southern California town called Santa Mira, in which everyone mysteriously turns stupid, flashes insincere smiles, and votes Republican. I am entering the realm of Robert Altman, this time in multicultural America.

Anyhow, the two litigious gals had gotten hold of the Chinese manager and were intent on torturing him until they got bored or had to return to work, whichever came first. They were talking NAACP, Anti-Defamation League, the

B'nai B'rith, the House Committee on Un-American Activities, the Food and Drug Administration, the Hemlock Society, the SPCA—they were going gangbusters. The kid was coming unglued. A middle-aged black guy eating his red-dye #2 chicken next to me read his newspaper, oblivious of the goings-on. Meanwhile, the manager, who had started out trying to reason with them along the lines of broccoli versus beef cost differential, had been reduced to a string of pathetic protests: "my job . . ." and "please try to understand" and "please don't." He was nearly in tears. The young ladies were plainly delighted, laughing uproariously, finally letting the manager off the hook with a "You're okay, man," and waving him off superciliously.

This helped my soul-sickness, but the ride back would take nearly an hour, and what with the rush hour starting up, I didn't know how long. That's when I remembered The Tower on Forty-seventh and the nearby Schnitzel joint. I saw the evening ahead taking shape. Not necessarily what I had in mind when I first stepped on the number 7, but given the imponderables that awaited me in El Cajon, along with my already delicate mental state, I felt secure for the first time that day I was heading in the right direction.

THE ZAM ZAM ROOM

The best bar in San Francisco reopened for business the other day under new management. But it's no good. They've got it all wrong. For one, the place is too bright and cheerful now. The new owners have installed all manner of lighting and cleaned up the mural over the bar. It looked better with sixty years of smoke stains, a kind of patina. Now, it just looks like what it is: a 1940 interior decorator's kitsch version of a magnified Persian miniature. If that weren't enough, the new owners have slapped a fresh coat of paint on the walls and put flowers all over the place—lilies, for crying out loud, gladioli, birds of paradise. Hideous. But worst of all, they keep the door open to the street, inviting all and sundry to come and take refreshment at the Persian Aub Zam Zam Room. That would have horrified Bruno more than anything else. A bat could have dwelled happily, day and night, in the original Zam Zam. If someone opened the door, especially in daylight, and hesitated before coming in, Bruno would shout, "Shut that door, there's a *stench* out there. Away with you, barbarian!"

Bruno Mooshei, sole proprietor and bartender, was famous for two things: his dry martinis and throwing people out of the bar. People from all over America, and even Europe, would come to the Zam Zam, sometimes for the martinis but usually to be thrown out. When David Letterman came to town to do a week of shows, his advance people phoned Bruno to see if he would throw Letterman out of the bar on the show. "No, I'm sorry, thank you," Bruno said over the phone. "Who's David Letterman?" he asked us. "I don't know this person. Why do these people bother me? He must be some New York person."

A New York person was not a good thing to be. Bruno found they tended to be noisy and self-regarding, and they always let you know they were from New York. Bruno, who was born in Baghdad and taken to the Bay Area as an infant, liked to boast that he'd never been east of Reno. He did admit once that he wouldn't mind "flying to Iowa and having a big, corn-fed steak. You know, just to see what it would be like." But the only time Bruno left town was to go to Reno to play keno and eat "extra heavy," or to visit family in Modesto. He'd never been on a jet and didn't like flying in general. "I went to Mexico once and was sick for eighteen years. Isn't that right, Ruth?" "That's right, Bruno," old Ruth would chime in from the corner stool.

I have always regarded it as one of the singular pieces of good fortune in my life that Bruno didn't throw me out when I first wandered into the Zam Zam twenty years ago. It was a small, dark, cavelike place with Moorish arches and decor. It took a few moments to adjust your eyes to the darkness. There was an old-fashioned vintage jukebox to the right with old-fashioned music playing, 1930s and 1940s big-band stuff. Bruno was at the far end of a 1940s-style, well-detailed semicircular bar with an old-fashioned vintage cash register. The whole place was old-fashioned vintage, including Bruno, who was chatting with a couple of friends. They all three glowered at me, hoping I might go away. It was one of the most depressing, unfriendly rooms I had ever walked into. I knew immediately I had found sanctuary.

I wasn't good for much at the age of thirty, but I could drink bourbon and I knew which bourbon I liked and how I liked it. Fortunately, it turned out to be one of the brands acceptable to Bruno. If you ordered Jack Daniel's, for instance, Bruno would tell you that you were more or less a fool, in thrall to Madison Avenue. Tanqueray gin and Chivas Regal also earned you a rough ride. But Old Grand-Dad was jake with Bruno, a good, unfashionable whiskey. So it was my order that saved me, and knowing to put my money on the plank before having to be asked. And then shutting up. Having another two in quick succession and leaving quietly, a modest tip behind, didn't hurt, either.

Who was allowed into the bar and who was thrown out was a celebrated topic of conversation among drinkers in San Francisco. In fact, it wasn't all that complex, at least on the surface. You took a seat on a stool at the bar, not at one of the tables in the back room. You had your money ready on the bar and you ordered your drink. This last had its hazards. Apart from the brands proscribed by Bruno (but which were nevertheless available), he held beer in low esteem. If you insisted, he would say, "I've got the horrible Budweiser, Beck's, and Heineken." Needless to say, if you ordered a Long Island Iced Tea or a Sex on the Beach, or even a margarita, he would throw you out. A bit of a minefield, but once you had it all figured out you were probably okay, unless Bruno just flat didn't like you or the way you looked.

Young, in general, was not a good look. Young female trumped male, but the young lady was supposed to be just that, a lady. Halter tops and nose rings didn't fly. Manners were big with Bruno. In his view, the "young today have no manners. I feel badly for their parents." Flash was never good. Bruno, who was Assyrian, referred to a certain type of patron who would wander into the bar from time to time as a "Hollywood sheikh." According to Bruno, a Hollywood sheikh was "someone from the Northeast. Inherited his money. Wears floppy collars with black alpaca sweaters. Drives a white Thunderbird with a redhead wearing a white leather jacket. Calls her 'tomato.'"

The Zam Zam was a great place to bring a woman, especially if you were an item or inclining in that direction. Bruno would give female customers a Zam Zam paper napkin with their drinks, and if he liked the look of them he would lean over the bar and offer up his Dickens martini joke: "What's a Dickens martini? Give up? No olive or twist."

The darkness and 1940s atmosphere lent the place a bit of mystery and romance. But it was the music on the jukebox that clinched it. Bruno went in for what's called "sweet-sounding society bands" or "hotel society music." There were some odd plays on the jukebox, like "Tales from the Vienna Woods" and excerpts from the *Victory at Sea* theme song, but it was the sweet music Bruno loved. "If there was more music like this," Bruno would say, leaning over the bar toward your date, "there would be less crime."

The prototype of the genre was Leo Reisman's orchestra,

which held a long residency at the stylish Central Park Casino in New York in the 1920s. This was the band that provided backing for some of Fred Astaire's biggest hits, like "Night and Day" and "Cheek to Cheek." In 1928, Reisman hired a handsome young piano player called Eddy Duchin (Peter's father). By 1931, with his matinee-idol looks and pianistic flourishes, Duchin had formed an orchestra of his own, replaced Reisman at the Central Park Casino, and become a national celebrity. Years later he was played by Tyrone Power in *The Eddy Duchin Story*, but the piano playing in the movie was done not by Duchin (of whom one sideman remarked, "He was the only musician I've ever known who could play a thirty-two-bar solo with thirty-two mistakes and receive an ovation") but by a young man named Carmen Cavallaro, Duchin's relief pianist. There was an awful lot of Carmen Cavallaro on the Zam Zam jukebox, with his fiddles and silky reeds, playing "Dancing in the Dark" or "I Didn't Know What Time It Was." It was a treat sitting there in the dark with your girl, a couple of drinks in you, listening to that swill with all its flourishes, glissandos, accelerandos, and the rest.

It was all part of a lost-era atmosphere that Bruno cultivated. The place was like a miniature of an old movie palace, with its darkness and exotic motifs. For Bruno, the bar was a piece of old San Francisco, a place that no longer existed except in films, photographs, and Dashiell Hammett novels. "There were only two great cities in the world," Bruno liked to say, "and both of them are gone: San Francisco and Shanghai. They were international and everyone dressed right."

Dressing right was big with Bruno. He always wore a vest, specially made to accommodate his girth, a tie and monogrammed shirt, also custom-made, with cuff links. He wanted his bar to have class, like in the old days. "Another perfect masterpiece, just like downtown," Bruno would say, shining a small flashlight on a freshly poured martini for the drinker to admire the surface tension keeping the cold, glistening libation from spilling over. "Of course," he would inevitably continue, "that's when we had a downtown. I'm talking about the 1930s and 1940s, when San Francisco was a real city with a real downtown. Women wore gloves and hats and could wait for a streetcar at 1 a.m. and no one would bother them."

Bruno's martinis were famous enough to catch the attention of the national press on several occasions. He mixed Boord's gin and Boissiere vermouth, in a ratio, he claimed, of one thousand to one. These were stirred, not shaken, and poured into ice-cold three-ounce glasses. "A couple of martinis is the first course of any good meal," Bruno liked to say, "just before the soup." Bruno himself, during an evening behind the bar, would down shots of his house bourbon in order to maintain his spirits. He called these quick tipples "shotskis" and might enjoy eight or ten on a typical work night. When he was in good cheer and had a few shotskis under his belt and was surrounded by regular patrons, he would often hold forth. He had a number of routines or riffs. A characteristic one went like this:

> Who was that actress, you know, she played in *Lifeboat*? Her father was the House Speaker from Alabama. She had such a Southern name. No, not Gloria Swanson. Tallulah. That's it,

Tallulah Bankhead. I saw her on Geary Street one night. I just walked by this woman in furs. She was stiff. Boiled as an owl. Boy, is that a Southern name or what! She talked like her mouth was full of marbles.

Then there was the "ten ugliest people" routine. "I'm number three," Bruno would say with pride. Topping the list was a professional wrestler from an earlier era, the French Angel. The Angel was afflicted with a glandular condition that renders its victims Neanderthal in appearance. On one occasion the Angel, a highly intelligent and well-educated man whose real name was Maurice Tillet, was asked to pose dressed as a caveman, with axe and loincloth, amid a group of reconstructed Neanderthal men in a local natural history museum. He was so convincing that he remained lost among the wax figures until, at a given signal, he plunged forward with an unearthly howl. This would have been an attention grabber. The rest of the list consisted of sports and showbiz personalities and politicians. I can't tell you their names because Bruno would have preferred me not to. "Except for four of us, we're all nice people," Bruno said, "just ugly."

I have heard Haight Street described as the cloaca of San Francisco. It surely has competition, but after nine at night, the description does not seem unfair. The sidewalks are filled with homeless, the drunk and drug-addicted, and the itinerant population attached to the halfway houses that the city bestowed on the Haight years ago. A late stroll down Haight between Stanyan and Central on any given evening will not recommend any homilies about the triumph of the human spirit.

The street long ago lost its coherence as part of a neighborhood. There is no bank or druggist, no butcher's shop. It has become a shopping and tourist area made up chiefly of thrift clothing and shoe stores, gift shops, and cheap beaneries. Haight Street caters to a young weekend crowd that pours in from the suburbs with their tattoos and piercings and Daddy's money. During the week, except in summer, it's a sleepy, unremarkable strip: part hippie theme park, part Desolation Row. If any of these kids wandered into the Zam Zam, Bruno would say, "Away with you, urchins. Go back to Novato and play basketball hoops in your driveway."

Bruno was raised on Haight Street. His father first had a tiny restaurant with five stools called the Pall Mall and then, in 1941, opened the Zam Zam. It was a successful bar, open seven days and nights a week, with two bartenders and barmaids on hand. The Haight has always had a carnival or fairground aspect to it. Golden Gate Park begins at the foot of it, and Haight Street was the point of departure for the Sutro Baths, where ocean water was fed into a Crystal Palace–type enclosure, and assorted entertainments on the city's western edge. Kezar Stadium, where the SF 49ers played their Sunday football games for many years, is only a few blocks west.

According to Bruno, the street changed in 1966. Bruno always blamed it on the *Miranda* decision, which required police to inform arrestees of their rights, and Chief Justice Earl Warren, on whose death Bruno closed the bar and went off to celebrate. In the mid-to-late 1960s the city, and the Haight in particular, became a catch basin for kids from all over the country who, lured by stories in *Time* and *Newsweek*, wanted to be part of the hippie adventure. The crush of new visitors can't have been a very palatable spectacle to those already in middle age who had been raised on Haight Street with its milliner and dry-goods shop, when everyone knew one another and would stop to chat, discuss the weather, or gossip about that Italian boy who plays baseball, DiMaggio, who was still hanging around the bank at closing time, trying to get a date with pretty Mary Ann DiMeeko.

How Bruno managed to survive the 1960s and early 1970s always mystified us. Business suffered, but by then his family had bought the building so he wouldn't have rent to worry about, and he would have had some income from the residential flats upstairs, in one of which he lived with his mother. But how on earth did he manage with the hippies and their Jesus hair, tatterdemalion outfits, and blissed-out smiles? "Oh, those people," Bruno would say, pointing to his arm, "they didn't drink; they all used dope." It wouldn't have been as simple as that. The Persian Aub Zam Zam Room would have been a great place to hang on acid, not least with Bruno as master of ceremonies. I suspect he simply threw them out, one after another, for years, as he continued to do with others long after the nature of Haight Street had changed.

Bruno was not a physically imposing presence. He was short and fat, but he could look menacing, especially if you didn't know him, like a swarthy Assyrian version of Edward G. Robinson, with maybe a gat under the bar, or at least a club or blackjack. He had none of these things, so far as I could tell. Instead, he had developed a science of removal. In retrospect, I don't think this was so much a result of his curmudgeonly nature, which was genuine and extreme, but rather his way of keeping the bar manageable for himself as sole bartender, and also of maintaining a particular atmosphere. The Zam Zam was a controlled environment and Bruno Mooshei controlled it, imperiously and often arbitrarily. His techniques were various. Here are a few:

This is just an old saloon. The corner bar's your best bet. They're new. They have lights. Modern music. It's the finest bar on the street.

I'm sorry, the tables are closed. There's no room. Do you understand English? They have been closed since seven-thirty. C-L-O-S-E-D.

Please, please, don't try to match wits with me. I try to serve people but they don't know how to order. One time I had to serve twelve martinis, one at a time. I can't do it anymore. I'm old. I'm senile. It's not you, it's me. I can't do it anymore. I'm sorry. You'll have to go drink somewhere else.

You've had too much to drink already. Go look after yourself, get a cup of coffee and a sandwich.

Hey, I don't want any of that in here. This is a bar. You two go find yourselves a motel room.

If you're going to sit in the horrible back room, take a table for two. Sorry, I don't serve here; this is for seated customers. I'm sorry. I have to work here. I need the room. Who are these people? Only people from Indiana sit in the horrible back room.

What do you mean, how much are the drinks? They're the same they've always been, or at least since I changed the price.

Young people. You have no class. I'm glad I'm on the two-yard line and will be dead soon. I can't take it anymore.

Bruno was a great trencherman. When he wasn't eating he liked to talk about food. Every Sunday he went to a rotten Italian restaurant out on the avenues and had prime rib. He had prime rib fifty-two Sundays a year. When he went to Reno it was as much for the huge, inexpensive hotel buffets as the keno. He liked to *analyze* the people in Reno—that's what he called it. "I've spent a lifetime analyzing corruption," he would say. He called the old ladies up in Reno "good morning, dears." A "good morning, dear," by definition, eats for breakfast "melba toast, cottage cheese, and pears, with a cherry on top." Every December Bruno made the same New Year's resolution: drink more, smoke extra heavy, and eat more animal fat. And unlike most, he kept to it.

Bruno was married twice, the first time very briefly right after the war. Of that wife he would say only, "Oh, the ogre. She was bad, very bad." He married again in his late sixties to a woman twenty-five years younger called Debbie. She was an alert, direct, full-figured woman, working-class and local, like Bruno. He adored her. Bruno would just about leave his feet when she walked into the bar. She, for reasons that eluded us, seemed to love Bruno. Then one day, only a year or so after they were married, Debbie had a brain aneurysm and dropped dead. Bruno kept the bar open and sighed a lot for a couple of years. "Oh, boy," he would say to no one in particular. It was difficult to watch. Bruno, over the years, had a ringside seat as all of us passed through our own vicissitudes, amatory and otherwise. None of us would have ever discussed a personal crisis with Bruno or vice versa. It was a very male place, for all the women who wandered through. It was also a conspicuously unarty environment. People associated with the arts did go there, but the only ones who were welcome operated under the same principle as gays in the military: don't ask, don't tell. You could discuss movies, if they weren't foreign or egghead films; and even books, on occasion, if they were about sports, cars, or World War II. Bruno had been a Navy corpsman at Guadalcanal. He learned over time that I was a poet. It was a mild source of embarrassment for us both. Alcohol helped.

Bruno tended bar solo for thirty-five years or so. With his big attitude, throwing people out all the time, dissing them, I often wondered why some cowboy didn't just vault over the bar and throttle him. Bruno maintained that he was frightened on only three occasions at the bar:

> She was black as her hair and with purple eyes. Ordered Miller and a shot of Dewar's with a British accent and I knew it was okay.

> Indian from Montana. Hair like a horse's tail. Tall. One-forty a.m. No one in the bar. Professor at Stanford. "Grandmother didn't want to, but we had to get rid of Custer."

> Ducktail. Leather jacket. Looked like a robber. Asked for a green Chartreuse.

I spent so much of my life over the past twenty years in that dark little room between the hours of five and six, talking about the ball game, listening to Glen Gray and the Casa Loma Orchestra play "It's the Talk of the Town," that I find it strange, disquieting even, to be about in the world now at that hour, left to my own devices. Of course, away from the confines of the Zam Zam Room, one can observe, among other things, the weather and change of light, not a small thing in this part of San Francisco where the fog moves in across Twin Peaks and breaks up among the hills.

Bruno liked the fog. He said, "Shirts feel better. Food tastes better." Bruno didn't care much for the sun or heat. He looked a little like a deep-sea creature out of his element when you saw him in the sunshine wearing casual clothes. If Bruno were a plant, you'd have to feed him lots of cigarette smoke, liquor, and red, fatty meat if you wanted him to flourish and bloom.

After Carmen Cavallaro and hotel society music, Bruno's next favorite was Fats Waller. There was a lot of Fats on the jukebox. I think Bruno found in Fats a kindred spirit: anarchic, boozy, and, well, fat. Bruno knew every song on that jukebox, as you might guess, having pretty much lived in that bar his entire adult life. He didn't exactly sing along with Fats as much as call out some of Fats's signature asides, like, "Keep it good, momma, ummmmmmm," "Don't give your right name," "Drag your body over here," "Oh, what a half pint would do."

One could keep track of the seasons while sitting at the Zam Zam, roughly. There was a transom over the door and a couple of small tinted-glass panels built into the doors. For instance, you could tell it was winter because it was dark outside and cold as hell in the bar. (Bruno didn't believe in heat.) Also, it would probably be raining. You knew it was May or October because it was bright outside. But there was a period of only a week or so in high summer when the light came through the transom and puddled on the floor in a particular way. I'll always remember that. I imagine it must be like that in certain prisons, with only a small patch of sky visible through the bars. A guy serving twenty years to life would come to treasure little details like that.

AN ENCYCLOPEDIC

HISTORY OF THE WORLD

Phoenix's Sky Harbor International Airport at 10 p.m. Doesn't look too goddamn international to me. The cocktail lounge gated up, the Nada Cantina likewise. A vaguely Southwest design motif in the carpet. *The New York Times* sold out. The local paper, *The Arizona Republic*, trumpets a "Steven Seagal Film Festival" at the top of its front page. The names of old cowboy towns coming over the public address system: "Final call for Durango, now boarding at gate number three." CNN on the TVs in the various waiting lounges. *USA Today* spread all over the plastic seats. The entire nation sucking from the same teat, a teat with a Nike swoosh and dripping Diet Coke.

Inexplicably, the notion of "wife-swapping country" comes into my head. True, sexual reverie is never far afield, but its expression can take on unpredictable manifestations. I'm visualizing convention gatherings at the Best Western and Comfort Inn. Forty-year-old couples exchanging Polaroids of themselves and their sport-utility vehicles over the Internet. All of them meeting months later in the VIP lounge of the hotel dressed in tight sporty outfits, reeking of perfume and cologne.

● ● ●

The puddle jumper that'll take us up to Flagstaff is a Beech-craft 1900, a prop. Once we're aloft, the fatigue, sourness, and trepidation magically drop away and I experience a kind of exultation, a godlike sense of mastery and well-being as the plane dips its starboard wing and heads north across the electrified plains of the Phoenix suburbs into the darkness of hills and small mountains of Precambrian gneiss, schist, and granite, the small mesas capped with lava flows and then up toward the ancient formations of the Central Highlands: the flaky silvery schist of metamorphic rock, the gruss and quartzite, racked and faulted rock nearly a mile wide. A mountain range on the scale of the Himalayas existed here 1.7 billion years ago when the Arizona region drifted south-eastward against another crustal plate and buckled the earth. Now it is nearly completely eroded.

But, of course, I don't really have any inkling whatsoever of what's down there as we fly over the Verde Valley toward Sedona with its red sandstone and buttes, a magical place now inundated by rich woo-woos, chiefly from California, and gurus in designer white linen outfits and seventy-five-dollar haircuts, a place where there are fourteen bookstores, twelve of them devoted to New Age titles. And finally to Flagstaff at seven thousand feet on the Colorado Plateau. I'm here to visit a high school, give a reading, and see the Grand Canyon. I wonder briefly what it would have been like for nineteenth-century imaginations such as Coleridge's, Keats's, John Clare's, to be suddenly aloft in a Beech-craft 1900, flying over London at night and out to sea. Or low over Paris. Or up over the Apennines. Surely something like this must have occurred early in the last century, with nineteenth-century characters finding themselves several thousand feet in the air, considering a perspective beyond imagining.

Grand Canyon: Nothing quite prepares you for it. Terror, that's what it's about. Not the hundreds of scenic photos, paintings, film clips. It will not be colonized psychologically. It defeats language. It defeats art. It is the most inhuman spectacle I have ever been confronted by.

At its base, down along the Colorado River, are the smooth, dark schists of the Vishnu group, intruded by Zoroaster marble. These rocks are two billion years old and at one point were buried under twelve miles of vertical rock. The buttes and hoodoos rising from the bottom of the canyon and sculpted by the wind beggar the biomorphic shapes of Brancusi, Hepworth, and Moore. When the scouts of Francisco Coronado's expedition came across it in 1540, they probably just backed slowly away and got the hell out of there. No white man came back for 236 years.

Phoenix: What a hellhole, makes downtown Providence look like Florence. Florence, Italy.

LAX: Me and my big mouth, episode #1,326. At the bar, having finished my Wolfgang Puck minipizza. Watching a basketball game on the TV overhead. A tall, attractive, somewhat hard-looking woman in her early thirties engages me in conversation. Where am I going? New Zealand. That doesn't grab her. Might as well have told her I sell plastic watchbands wholesale and am headed to San Jose. I ask her, not thinking, "Which airline do you fly for?" "Is it really that obvious?" she asks, clearly angered and hurt. "Uh, ha ha, no, of course not. It's just your outfit . . ." (black slacks, black blazer, sensible shoes). That really does it. She turns 180 degrees to the guy on her other side. No matter, my flight leaves in forty minutes, anyhow.

Aloft: A United Airlines 747 stretch, 485 passengers. An aisle seat next to a dopey-looking young Aussie couple. Nike products head to toe. Already going to fat, these two are really going to be looking like shit in twenty years, right around the time their kids are headed off to college. Twelve hours to Auckland, direct. The flight plan will take us over Christmas Island at the equator, over Pago Pago in American Samoa, and into Auckland 10 a.m. Sunday. It is 11 p.m. on Friday, March 6. A kind woman in Phoenix, as prearranged, will send me the front page of *The Arizona Republic* for Saturday, March 7, lest I miss anything. And I shall read it, exactly one month later, on April 7 in San Francisco: the usual larceny, mayhem, and sports scores.

After two rotten movies, and a Hobson's choice between chicken-something and beef-something, the cabin has slipped collectively into fitful slumber, John Grisham novels lying open on their tummies, the younger couples curled sweetly toward one another. Can't sleep. Walk to the back of the plane by the heads and emergency door. A fatso from up near Bodega Bay in west Marin, voluble as all get-out and stinking of booze, is well into some large *histoire* or other to a poor New Zealander, obviously trapped and whose manners are too good to blow the gasbag off. Out of the tiny window of the door only darkness.

There's a poem by James Dickey called "Falling," an over-heated extravaganza filled with the weighty tropes and psychological drama of that era. But the idea of the poem has stayed in my mind over the years. Its epigraph is from a newspaper story of the time:

> A 29-year-old stewardess fell . . . to her death tonight when she was swept through an emergency door that suddenly sprang open . . . The body . . . was found . . . three hours after the accident.

The young woman in the poem falls into a cornfield in Kansas with her skirt over her head and takes nearly two hundred very slow lines to get there. Should the door fly open right now and I am sucked into space, down toward the mighty Pacific, I might well land, after considerable and concentrated reflection, with a stupendous thud on the atoll called Christmas Island.

Way down there, 220 years before, Captain Cook, heading north from a most enjoyable stay in Tahiti, crossed the equator in longitude 156° west on the night of December 22–23, and on the 24th, shortly after daybreak, spotted land. It was a barren atoll, the largest of all atolls in the area, with an anchorage on the lee side. Cook was seventeen months out of Plymouth, England, at the time. He had asked his Tahitian hosts if they knew of any islands to the north or northwest, and they did not. The Spanish galleons that had made the run between Acapulco and Manila for the previous two hundred years had never reported any land in those two areas. Thus, Christmas was gratefully celebrated and the atoll given its name. Cook and his men procured great numbers of green turtles for their further passage. Two of the crew somehow managed to get lost on the flat, almost bare island, nearly perishing in the heat, surviving only on turtle blood until they were found.

The cabin begins waking up as we fly over the Tonga Trench, crossing the International Date Line at 180° longitude. I'm presented with something egglike accompanied by a sausage. The third and final movie begins: *Home Alone III*. If the plane popped a sprocket right now and dropped 32,000 feet to the ocean, it would continue to sink another 35,433 feet into the Tonga Trench, which could accommodate not only us but twelve Grand Canyons as well. I speculate about my young neighbors' sex life as they begin to stir, but only briefly.

The Maoris came to New Zealand more than one thousand years ago from Tahiti, in voyaging canoes. First, they traveled one hundred miles to Huahine, a neighbor of Raiatea, the island associated with Hawaiki, their legendary home. They then traveled five hundred miles southwest to Rarotonga, where they would have rested and reprovisioned for the sixteen-hundred-mile open-sea voyage to New Zealand. The canoes were twin-hulled, about fifty to seventy-five feet in length, and they could hold up to one hundred men. They steered by reading the swells and waves, by the clouds, the sun, and the stars, among which are the Magellanic Clouds, two faint opalescent galaxies that revolve around the South Pole. The canoes, loaded, could make about 100 to 150 miles a day. They were lashed by coconut fiber and sennit and caulked with breadfruit sap. They carried two sails and an outrigger float. They could be provisioned for up to a month with fermented breadfruit, pounded taro, and coconuts. The voyagers caught fish and ate them raw. They drank rainwater. In a month they could travel up to forty-five hundred miles, or across all of Polynesia, from Easter Island to New Zealand.

The Maoris tend to run big, large, and extra-large. They love tattoos, and they love to fight best of all. Darwin was not impressed with them when he visited on the *Beagle*; he found them a big letdown after Tahiti. "Both their persons and their houses are filthy dirty," he observed, also noting, "I should think a more warlike race of inhabitants could not be found in any part of the world." The Maoris had greeted Captain Cook sixty years before Darwin by throwing stones and shouting, "Come on shore and we will kill you and eat you all." Subsequently, the Maoris came out in canoes to attack Cook and his crew. They were shot down by musket fire but continued coming, throwing rocks when they ran out of spears, fish when they ran out of rocks.

Darwin made amused mention of a custom the Maoris had that he called "rubbing noses":

> The women, on our first approach, began uttering something in the most dolorous voice, they then squatted down and held up their faces; my companion standing over them, one after another, placed the bridge of his nose at right angles to theirs

and commenced pressing. This lasted rather longer than a cordial shake of the hand with us; and as we vary the force of the hand shaking, so do they in pressing. During the process they uttered comfortable little grunts, very much as two pigs do when rubbing against each other.

"What a curious place for a tattoo," I say to her.
"You are very hairy," she says to me.

New Zealand has 3,500,000 people and 67,000,000 sheep, which inspires barroom jokes like "Hey, McCloud, get offa my ewe."

More enduring music, painting, and literature came out of the area in New York City encompassing the zip codes 10009 to 10014 in the winter of 1959 than has come out of New Zealand in 150 years.

The Maori had no name for themselves until the English arrived, eventually calling themselves *Maori*, which means "normal."

New Zealanders have almost no interest whatsoever in the outside world. Perhaps because they are a day ahead of whatever happens. The main newspaper has half a column on the fourth page devoted to "The World."

> My life here is not disagreeable. I have a great resource in the piano, and a little employment in teaching. Then I go to Mrs. Taylor's and astonish the poor girl with calling her favourite parson a spoon . . .

It is a pity that you don't live in this world, that I might entertain you about the price of meat . . .

I have now told you everything I can think of except that the cat's on the table and I'm going to borrow a new book to read—no less than an account of all the systems of philosophy of modern Europe.

(From a letter written by Mary Taylor to her friend
Charlotte Brontë in 1845, five years after the
founding of the small settlement of Wellington.)

Manhattan: Two friends are walking down the street, one of whom, an out-of-towner, asks his friend, "Why does the pavement here seem so much harder than anywhere else?" To which his friend responds, "Because Manhattan is built on a shelf of solid rock that goes all the way down to hell."

New Jersey: I go to the post office to mail a package to New Zealand. The TV is going overhead. The window clerks are watching a show hosted by a genial fat woman named Rosie. Rosie has several children on the show and she is sniffing their sneakers to determine which one smells the worst. "How bad can a little girl's feet smell?" one clerk asks another.

When young people from Phoenix or New Zealand move to New York and begin to take on the identity of New Yorkers, the first thing they learn to say, in order to affirm their superiority to outsiders or those freshly arrived, is "It's not called the Avenue of the Americas. It's Sixth Avenue."

The second thing they learn to say is "What, are you from Jersey or something?"

Part Three

NO ANTONIN ARTAUD WITH

THE FLAPJACKS, PLEASE

Readers may remember how the U.S. military blared Van Halen and others at the Panamanian dictator Manuel Noriega when he took refuge in the Vatican Embassy in Panama City during our invasion of Panama years ago. This method of rousting the wicked proved so successful that it was repeated during the recent Afghan experience, when heavy-metal chart-busters were unleashed on caves thought to be sheltering Taliban and al-Qaeda fighters. The English newspaper *The Guardian* reported last year that we were breaking the wills of captured terrorists, or suspected terrorists, by assaulting them first with heavy metal, followed by "happy-smiley children's songs." The real spirit-cruncher turns out to be the Barney "I Love You" song played for hours on end. Even the most hardened, sadistic killers buckle under "that kind of hell," or so asserted a reliable source. But if that fails to work, I suggest a round-the-clock tape of Garrison Keillor reading poems on his daily *Writer's Almanac* show.

Now, had Keillor not "strayed off the reservation" and kept to his *Prairie Home Companion* show with its Norwegian bachelor farmers and Lutheran bake sales (a sort of *Spoon River Anthology* as presented by the Hallmark Hall of

Fame), comfort food for the philistines, a contemporary, bittersweet equivalent to *The Lawrence Welk Show* of years past, I'd have left him alone. But the indefatigable and determined purveyor of homespun wisdom has wandered into the realm of fire, and for his trespass must be burned.

If it were up to me, I'd suggest we borrow the U.S. military's tactics and lock Mr. Keillor in a Quonset hut, crank up the speakers, and give him an industrial-strength dose of, say, Albert Ayler saxophone solos until this "much-beloved radio personality" forswears reading poems over the airwaves every morning. Ayler's music is not a particular enthusiasm of mine. The late poet Ted Joans called Ayler's solos as shocking as hearing someone scream "Fuck!" in St. Patrick's Cathedral in New York. But Garrison Keillor could do with a little Albert Ayler in his church, and church is what Keillor is all about. Everything that comes out of his mouth in that treacly baritone, which occasionally releases into a high-pitched, breathless tremolo when he wants to convey emotion, is a sermon. The homily runs something like this: We are good, if foolish and weak, and may gain redemption through compassion, laughing at ourselves, and bad poetry badly read.

Albert Ayler could only be a tonic for Keillor—a tonic we will force-feed him as they force-feed a goose in Périgord for foie gras—because Ayler's art is opposite to Keillor's shtick. Everything Keillor does is about reassurance, containment, continuity. He makes no demands on his audiences, none whatsoever. To do so would only be bad manners. Gentleness and good manners are the twin pillars of the church of Keillor.

Ayler is all about excess, anger, challenge, exploration, risk. Even when his improvisations fail, they fail bravely. His mission is to explode conventions and expectations. It would never have crossed his mind musically to be ingratiating or reassuring or polite. Nor should it have done. That is not what music or poetry is for, especially in times like these. There is a passage from a William Carlos Williams poem, "Asphodel, That Greeny Flower," dear to the hearts of those who would peddle poetry, or the idea of poetry, to the masses. I have heard it read on NPR in that solemn, hushed tone that is a commonplace among poetry salespersons, not least Mr. Keillor:

> Of asphodel, that greeny flower,
>   I come, my sweet,
>   to sing to you!
> My heart rouses
>   thinking to bring you news
>   of something
> that concerns you
>   and concerns many men. Look at
>   what passes for the new.
> You will not find it there but in
>   despised poems.
>   It is difficult
> to get the news from poems
>   yet men die miserably every day
>   for lack
> of what is found there.

A pretty sentiment, to be sure, but simply untrue, as anyone who has been to the supermarket or ballpark recently will concede. Ninety percent of adult Americans can pass through this life tolerably well, if not content, eating, defecating, copulating, shopping, working, catching the latest Disney blockbuster, without having a poem read to them by Garrison Keillor or anyone else. Nor will their lives be diminished by not standing in front of a Cézanne at the art museum or listening to a Beethoven piano sonata. Most people have neither the sensitivity, the inclination, nor the training to look or listen meaningfully, nor has the culture encouraged them to, except with the abstract suggestion that such things are good for you. Multivitamins are good for you. Exercise, fresh air, and sex are good for you. Fruit and vegetables are good for you. Poetry is not.

Especially most of what Garrison Keillor reads on his *Writer's Almanac*, which, as a rule, isn't poetry at all but prose arbitrarily broken into lines masquerading as poetry. The typical Keillor selection tends to be anecdotal, wistful: more often than not a middle-aged creative writing instructor catching a whiff of mortality in the countryside—watching the geese head south, getting lost in the woods, this sort of thing.

John Ash, writing of the brilliant fellow English poet Roy Fisher, speaks of Fisher's "rage, his refusal to be politely depressed." There is a virulent strain of the "politely depressed" in American poetry. There are other, equally obnoxious and resistant strains, but the "politely depressed" is a pertinacious little bugger, and Garrison Keillor is only helping to spread it.

Poetry not only isn't good for you, bad poetry has been shown to cause lymphomas and, in extreme instances, pancreatic cancer in laboratory experiments. (I'll have to dig around in my notes to find exactly what study that was . . .) I avoid Keillor's poetry moment at 9 a.m. here in San Francisco as I avoid sneezing, choking, rheumy-eyed passengers on the streetcar, lest I catch something. But occasionally, while surfing for the news, I get bit and am nearly always sickened, if not terminally, for several hours.

Keillor means well. Of course he does. That's his problem. His execrable *Almanac* begins with a few bars of hymn-style piano. And how could it be otherwise? We are in church. Garrison is ministering culture. A series of four or five capsulized, and trivialized, biographies of writers born on that same day follows: "Emily Dickinson was born on this day in 1830 in Amherst, Massachusetts. She wasn't a picture, God knows, and was reclusive in her ways. She wrote small, puzzling poems that no one read until she was dead." Keillor then proceeds to read a poem, of Ms. Dickinson's, if we are lucky, or of one of his standbys like Billy Collins, if we are not. It doesn't really matter. Keillor embalms whatever poem he reads within the burnished caul of his delivery, a voice one friend of mine describes as "probably taken out at day's end and left to stand all night in a glass of bourbon." Keillor then signs off: "Be well, do good work, keep in touch." You bet, Garrison, I'm right on it.

I have little doubt that a Keillor staffer picks the poems for the show, a superannuated former MFA from the Iowa workshop would be my guess, one familiar with Keillor's appalling taste, sentimentality, and the constraints of format. Keillor will deny this, as will his staff. But there's no way he'd have the time, either to read poetry or even sift casually through volumes current and old, to choose an appropriate poem. He not only has his weekly radio show, he's busy producing rotten books on what seems an almost seasonal basis. Also, judging by the introduction to *Good Poems*, a selection of poems from five years of those read on *The Writer's Almanac*, Keillor is infatuated with the idea of poetry but knows and cares little or nothing about the art, what's good, what's bad, and how it's made. But that doesn't stop him, oh no. Keillor is all appetite, irrepressible, the hardest-working "thoughtful person" in show business.

In his introduction to the collection, Keillor warns us:

> The goodness of a poem is severely tested by reading it on the radio. The radio audience is not the devout sisterhood you find at poetry readings, leaning forward, lips pursed, hanky in hand [?!]; it's more like a high school cafeteria. People listen to poems while they're frying eggs and sausage and reading the paper and reasoning with their offspring, so I find it wise to stay away from stuff that is too airy or that refers offhandedly to the poet Li Po or relies on your familiarity with butterflies or Spanish or Monet.

"So I'll be feeding you mostly shit" is what Garrison could well go on to say. No Antonin Artaud with the flapjacks, please.

Actually, *Good Poems* isn't as bad as one might think had one been listening now and then to Keillor's morning segment over the years. Its principal virtue is that one doesn't have to endure Keillor's poetry voice. But the range of the selections suggests more variety than the show customarily offers, and there's a healthy dollop of Anonymous, Shakespeare, Ms. Dickinson, Burns, Whitman, et al. There are surprising and delightful choices I would never have credited Keillor in making (he probably didn't), like Anne Porter, an excellent and little-known poet published by the now extinct Zoland Press. And the volume contains enlightened selections of the work of well-known contemporaries; I'm thinking here of a particularly good C. K. Williams poem. Of course, on balance, it's a rotten collection I wouldn't recommend to anyone, but it's not so bad as it might have been.

Keillor is not the first to offer the masses reassurance and diversion through poetry on the radio. Edgar Guest (1881–1957) broadcast a weekly program on NBC from 1931 to 1942, and his topical verses were syndicated to over three hundred newspapers throughout the United States in his daily "Table Chat" column. Known as the "poet of the people," Guest published more than twenty volumes of poetry and was thought to have written over 11,000 poems, almost all of them fourteen lines long and presenting "a sentimental view of everyday life." Guest's *Collected Verse* appeared in 1934 and went into at least eleven editions. "I take the simple everyday things that happen to me," Guest wrote, "and I figure it happens to a lot of other people and I make simple rhymes out of them."

Are we not yet adult enough as a culture to acknowledge that the arts are not for everyone, and that bad art is worse than no art at all; and that good or bad, art's exclusive function is to entertain, not to improve or nourish or console, simply entertain? And in this, *Moby-Dick* or Bach's *Well-Tempered Clavier* are not different than the movie *The Cat in the Hat* or Britney Spears wiggling her behind onstage, the former being more complexly entertaining and satisfying, but only for those who can appreciate the difference, and they are the minority.

Let me quote from a lecture the British poet Basil Bunting gave in Vancouver in 1970:

> Poetry is no use whatever. The whole notion of usefulness is irrelevant to what are called the fine arts, as it is to many other things, perhaps to most of the things that really matter. We who call ourselves "the West," now that we've stopped calling ourselves Christians, are so imbued with the zeal for usefulness that was left us by Jeremy Bentham that we find it difficult to escape from utilitarianism into a real world.

In America, usefulness is indissolubly wed to profit, increased capital. Poetry is no exception. It is worth reflecting during National Poetry Month that creative writing, over the past forty years, has subsumed American poetry and become a $250 million industry, a rather seamy industry, and an offshoot of the rather seamy Human Potential Movement industry. American poetry is now an international joke. And not just internationally: American novelists, nonfiction writers, scholars, the enlightened general reader who a generation ago read poetry as a matter of course, for pleasure, rarely attend to it anymore. Poetry is seldom, if ever, reviewed in mainstream journals like *The New York Times*, *The New Yorker*, *Harper's*, *The Atlantic Monthly*, and when it is reviewed at all, it is reviewed in a cursory or inept manner.

Publishers will cheerfully volunteer—at least last time I checked—that poetry has never sold so well. Surely never have so many written it and sought to publish it. I have every expectation that Keillor's *Good Poems* is doing land-office business. It's that kind of book and has the editor's broad public appeal behind it. I expect Mr. Keillor's morning show has legions of faithful listeners as well, who feel nourished and broadened by his daily reading of poetry, as countless Americans once felt about Edgar Guest and his more homely product.

But I, for one, have never in my lifetime seen the situation of poetry in this country more dire or desperate. Nor is the future promising. Cultural and economic forces only suggest further devastation of any sort of vital literary culture, along with the prospects of the very, very few—it is always only a very few—poets who will matter down the road. What little of real originality is out there is drowning in the waste products spewing from graduate writing programs like the hog farm waste that recently overflowed its holding tanks in the wake of Hurricane Isabel, fouling the Carolina country-side and poisoning everything in its path.

Let me put it starkly: the better animals in the jungle aren't drawn to poetry anymore, and they're certainly not tuned in to Keillor's *Writer's Almanac*. Just as the new genre of the novel drew off most of the brilliant young writers of the nineteenth century, movies, television, MTV, advertising, rock 'n' roll, and the Internet have taken the best among the recent crop of young talent. Do you suppose for a moment that a spirited youngster with a brilliant, original mind and gifted up the yin-yang is going to sit still for two years of creative-writing poetry workshops presided over by a dispir-ited, compromised mediocrity, all the while critiquing and being critiqued by younger versions of the same?

Boosterism of the sort Garrison Keillor participates in on *The Writer's Almanac* will succeed in shifting more than a few books of poetry, not least his *Good Poems*, and in encouraging countless more people to write. But there exists a surfeit of encouragement of this kind in America at the moment, and there's very little to show for it. The merchandising of poetry, or at least the slick, sentimental idea of it, is the problem, not the solution.

Allow me to conclude with a poem called "National Poetry Day" by the Scottish poet Gael Turnbull, which is timely and also reminds us that this sort of foolishness, though endemic in the U.S. of A., is not altogether unique to it.

"Transform your life with poetry"
the card said, and briefly I fussed
that this overestimated the effect
until I remembered how it had thrust
several old friends,
plus near and dear,
into distress and penury,
how even I, without the dust
of its magic, might have achieved
peace of mind, even success,
so maybe the advice is just,
not to be ignored, a sort of timely
Health Warning from the Ministry
of Benevolence
at the Scottish Book Trust.

LUNCHING WITH GINSBERG

It would have been February 5, William Burroughs's birthday. Ginsberg was in a panic about having forgotten it (Burroughs's seventy-fifth)—only one among his several panics that gray, frigid Sunday afternoon on East Twelfth Street. Ginsberg's anxiety resembled that of a favored child loath to disappoint a loving parent. No, that wouldn't be quite it: Burroughs as a loving parent, no. Perhaps it was more Auntie Allen not wanting to let down his weird elderly nephew. There was a fair bit of the doting auntie in Allen Ginsberg.

It must have been 1989, which would have made Allen sixty-two years old at the time. Inside another eight or nine years he'd be dead, but he was looking reasonably good that particular day for an old beatnik. His liver got him in the end—an earlier bout with hepatitis developed into cancer. So the doctors surmised. He wasn't a drinker and I don't expect he was doing drugs at that stage. He didn't offer me a joint or a line of blow, at any rate. Besides, it was early in the day for any of that.

I was absorbed in taking in the apartment and the measure of the man. I'll let one of his biographers, Barry Miles, describe the setup:

In March 1975, Allen and Peter Orlovsky moved into a much larger apartment, on East Twelfth Street between First Av-

enue and Avenue A. It had six rooms, two of which were very
small, and had been created by knocking together two small
apartments, an arrangement that led, somewhat incongru-
ously, to Allen's having a sink right next to his desk in his
office. There were three south-facing front rooms ... with a
third becoming Allen's office. When Allen awoke in the morning, all he could see from the window was the top of the church
opposite, which, in the gray winter light, reminded him of his
days in Paris ... They painted the walls white, tacked their
picture of the young Rimbaud on the wall, and were home.
[*Ginsberg: A Biography*, p. 457]

More presently about Peter Orlovsky, who was no longer
Allen's roommate. But I remember immediately liking
Allen, somewhat to my surprise. He was nothing at all like
his cartoonish public persona. In fact, he reminded me of no
one so much as my old pediatrician and family friend, Sam
Prince. The two didn't resemble each other physically, nor
was there anything particular in the manner. I suppose he
was just very familiar to me: Jewish, north Jersey; both of us
provincials out of a very particular psychosocial milieu; ten
miles and twenty-three years apart, growing up in the same
light, the same benzene fumes. The same oil refinery fire-
eaters flaming the night along the Jersey Turnpike. The same
speech patterns, body language, and the rest. I was immediately comfortable around him. I could read him easily.

I suspect he felt the same. There was no pretense or awk-
wardness. There was no side to him, at least that I could see.
There was nothing either of us could do for or to the other.
We quickly relaxed into an afternoon's acquaintance. What
struck me first, I remember, was his seriousness and intelli-

gence. Poets, no matter how bright, tend to be silly, loose characters, self-involved and oblivious to the world around them. Somewhat like academics, in this last regard—which, in America, almost all poets are, thereby compounding the dilemma. Allen taught a couple of courses at Brooklyn College during those years, but he certainly wasn't recognizable as your conventional poet/academic. He was far too present and sharp, of the world. More like a businessman, really. Not the car salesman or insurance adjuster sort; more the investment banker type, I'd suggest. Or a physician. Which, I suppose, is why he reminded me of Dr. Prince. I doubt one thing has to do with another, but as poets we were both children of another New Jersey physician: William Carlos Williams.

Allen looked the lumpy old boho, but he was astute in that business or physician way, gracious in manner but tirelessly appraising, inquisitive. I found it flattering: that is, to be appraised by someone of that stature and not to be dismissed out of hand as a bore, a poseur, or an outright fool. Ginsberg was, in reality, the CEO of a considerable and enduring international enterprise: Allen Ginsberg, Inc. He had traveled the world, for the most part as a celebrity, and met all manner of people: Ezra Pound, Bob Dylan, lepers, you name it.

It was curiosity, not admiration, that brought me to look up Ginsberg. He had been a huge influence when I was in my late teens, as had been his friends: Kerouac, Corso, Snyder, Whalen, Burroughs, even poor Carl Solomon, whom Ginsberg had met during a brief incarceration in the madhouse. Collectively, this group was a marvelous tonic (at least to a seventeen-year-old) for the Lowell and New Critical miasma

of the period, with its self-conscious, elevated tone; its allu-
sions, ironies, formalist tricks; its insistence on being taken
seriously. The self-satisfied, conspicuously elegant poet
Anthony Hecht, who was much admired in academic circles and the recipient of a Pulitzer Prize, visited our high
school in 1966—on what was called Careers Day, a day put
aside for distinguished alumni to speak to men in the senior
classes about their vocations. I was quite definite about
wanting to be a poet by the time I was sixteen or so. Mr.
Hecht, with his vaguely English elocution (acquired in the
Bronx?) was definitely not what I had in mind.

I now think more of Ginsberg's achievement, at least early
in his career, than I did thirteen years ago. Back then, I
was probably at the tail end of my disillusionment with
the entire Beat enterprise. Also, I was contemptuous of the
way Ginsberg had shamelessly merchandised himself and
"the Beats" over the years, squandering his own gifts in
the process. I was contemptuous of his opportunistic hippie
Buddhism, his addiction to celebrity and celebrities, the infantile politics (which now strike me as more visionary than
infantile), his association with the silly and occasionally
sleazy Naropa Institute in Colorado and its Jack Kerouac
School of Disembodied Poetics. I was contemptuous of the
whole business of being Allen Ginsberg.

Of course, I'm older now, and, inevitably, less judgmental.
I have also observed, over time, how more *dignified, serious-
minded* poets have cultivated their reputations via the
critical-academic establishment—those tireless, decades-
long campaigns for Pulitzers, even the Nobel, with all the

bartering, double crosses, and leveraging that entails. Of course, this takes place behind the veneer of priestly devotion to the Art of Poesia, the life of the spirit and all that.

Ginsberg, at least, made no pretense about it. He was, figuratively, on the busiest street corner in town, jealous of his position there, and with his skirt up over his head, wiggling his hairy old ass for whatever it was worth.

But the private man was nothing like that, at least that particular afternoon. Sure, he could be self-absorbed, occasionally frantic, wheeling and dealing over the phone in an obnoxious humiliating fashion. But for the most part, I encountered a kind, thoughtful, soft-spoken man: a mensch. The frenzy, the self-aggrandizement, and all the rest seemed a long destructive war that had laid waste his poetry and, probably, any chance of emotional equilibrium or peace.

"Are you queer?" Allen asked pointedly, directly after we had been seated in a large, noisy Ukrainian restaurant around the corner. "No," I said, mildly taken aback, but certainly not mortified or feeling jumped. He famously was— and by all reports, at the age of thirty-nine I would not have been his type. He looked at me in his appraising way, not disbelieving me, I think, but probably gauging my reaction. "Just curious," he said matter-of-factly, and took a camera out of his satchel. He began photographing me, right there in the booth. "I hope you don't mind," he said. "I like to photograph people." I did mind, in fact. I dislike being photographed, particularly in a public place by a famous person. But he was mad for photographing and seemed to do it compulsively. He meant nothing by it, really. He's had shows of his photography, books and so on. It's not very interesting.

We enjoyed a pleasant, starchy lunch: the kasha and farfel, blintzes, kreplach, and the rest. Old-world Jew food, leaden, bland, with chicken fat (schmaltz) as a base, in lieu of butter or olive oil. A poor substitute, a substitute of the poor. But familiar to us both from our growing up. A cuisine like the British: dismal, unhealthy, somehow comforting.

On the way out of the restaurant, we encountered the most remarkable woman I had ever seen. At least six feet tall, very black, drop-dead gorgeous, with an Apache's cheekbones and a flattop hairdo—for all the world, like a savage Diana. She also looked very familiar, and she was also looking very long and hard at Allen, eyes narrowed in a not entirely friendly way. And he at her, very intently. This engagement of fierce stares continued for an uncomfortably long time, then suddenly disengaged, and off they went their separate ways, not quite satisfied. What had transpired was two celebrities, encountering one another at short range, recognizing each other as celebrities, but not knowing quite who the other was. Allen's celebrity has endured longer than Grace Jones's, but I have never seen such a dramatic-looking creature before or since. I can't imagine what I would do if I was sitting next to someone like that at a bar and she said, "Let's go to my place and fuck." Timidly follow, I suppose, or run off whimpering into the night.

Allen invited me back to his place for tea. It was a bitter-cold afternoon, raw in the particular way New York gets in late

January, early February. There are colder towns, and I've lived in a few, but cold doesn't get much meaner than it does in Manhattan, with that river wind blowing up the streets and swirling among the buildings. Besides, I was enjoying Allen's company.

There had been that moment when, leaving his apartment to go to lunch, he said: "Wait a minute. Let me just tell Peter I'm going to be gone for an hour or so." This was Peter Orlovsky, Allen's longtime companion, whom Allen had set up in an apartment next door to his. Allen knocked on the door, and no one answered for a long time. Allen kept saying, "Peter, Peter, it's me, Allen." Finally, after five or ten minutes of this, I heard shuffling, the unfastening of locks, and the door opened, at least as far as the chain allowed. Allen explained to a wild-eyed old man that he would be going to lunch with his friend August, and would return before too long. Orlovsky looked at me, looked at Allen, looked back at me, made an unfriendly animal sound, and, teeth bared, lurched forward, face first, through the space in the door, gargling and shrieking like an enraged beast.

Allen made gently disapproving and comforting noises all the while before, finally, closing the door on Peter. I'm not sure, but maybe Ginsberg had keys which worked from the outside that kept that lunatic in his cage. "Peter's a bit upset, it seems," Allen said sheepishly.

The two men were no longer lovers, but remained close, literally. Orlovsky had always been mad as a hatter. His entire family was mentally ill. My sister used to meet with Peter's brother Julius, when, as a psychiatric social worker, she was employed in the outpatient clinic at Bellevue. Peter would sometimes show up as well. Now Peter's dementia had been aggravated by alcoholism and, apparently, someone was getting cocaine to him now and again. Which wouldn't have helped. When they first moved to Twelfth Street, Allen, Peter, and Peter's girlfriend Denise all shared the same apartment. This arrangement had altered over time. I cannot imagine the Orlovsky I met in 1989 cohabiting with a woman, Denise or anybody else. But allegedly he did, at least now and then. Alcohol notwithstanding, it probably wasn't a cocktail party in that apartment, with Katharine Hepburn and Cary Grant in a scintillating quipping match. More like a rabid wolverine and its mate.

The remainder of the afternoon unfolded like a play, or a movie—a rather depressing movie, I should think. Along the lines of Bergman, but artless. There does exist a faux cinema verité film of Ginsberg and his pals from 1957 which is not half bad, titled *Pull My Daisy*, shot by the estimable photographer Robert Frank and "produced" by the then abstract expressionist painter Alfred Leslie. It's now nearly impossible to get hold of, due to litigation between Frank and Leslie.

The film is loosely based on the third act of a play Kerouac wrote, originally titled *The Beat Generation*. Kerouac doesn't appear in the film, but delivers a voiceover narration. The whole thing has an improvisational feel to it, much of it successful, or at least amusing. Ginsberg, Corso, and Orlovsky, essentially, are playing themselves. The plot is flimsy, but the antics of the youthful Ginsberg and his friends, including the painter Larry Rivers playing the Kerouac character, have a merry, almost Dada feel. I somehow don't think

Tristan Tzara, Hugo Ball, and Kurt Schwitters were in the minds of the author and players, but no matter. The rather dour Swiss-born Robert Frank (best known for his realist photographs that make up *The Americans*) had a fascination with the Beats, in many respects his opposite, at least temperamentally. Regardless, his original camerawork and direction pull the film together and provide a rhythm to all the shenanigans. The memory of Allen's apartment that afternoon would strike me forever after as the ruins of *Pull My Daisy*.

I don't remember the exact sequence of phone calls and events after we returned from lunch. Nor the specifics of our conversation, apart from Allen introducing me to a primitive form of the blues, the one-stringed slide guitar—in this instance, judging by the record sleeve, played by a derelict-looking older black man on a street corner in L.A. Allen taught a course on the blues at Brooklyn College, and seemed to have a real feeling for the music. I half suspect all his dopey chanting, the tiny cymbals and childish songs (meant, I guess, to be in the spirit of Blake), was a surrogate, his way of singing the blues. I found it embarrassing, perhaps at moments endearing. We certainly didn't discuss poetry.

But not long after we got back, the phone began ringing. I seem to remember Orlovsky screaming and pounding next door, but that soon blended into the ambient noise. Perhaps the first call was the one from Cape Breton Island, off Nova Scotia. I had to piece bits together, but on the other end of the line was a former director of the Naropa Institute—one of the shady ersatz swamis associated with the place who hadn't worked out too well and somewhere along the line had contracted AIDS, of which he was now dying.

It was a one-way conversation for the most part, Allen throughout making periodic thoughtful-sounding grunts and acknowledgments. This went on for quite some time. The man on the other end was almost certainly hysterical, probably screaming somethng like "I'm going to fucking DIE, dammit," or so I interpreted from the expression on Allen's face. Allen listened, nodding, grunting, patient for a long while, until finally, cutting short the conversation, he said, "Well, what we've got here is a real koan, don't we?" A koan is, approximately, an insoluble Zen riddle, a metaphysical puzzle with no answer. This is not how I would have characterized his friend's dilemma. It left the poor man out of his mind with frustration, rage, and disbelief, not that there was anything helpful Allen could really have said. The conversation was concluded. Allen's Buddhism, I surmised, served him as a handy tool for any number of awkward occasions.

Allen did not seem in any way upset by this conversation, and we quickly settled back into our own desultory exchange. I do recall Allen was inquisitive and I was forthcoming. That was probably the conversation dynamic. I enjoyed the frankness of the to and fro. He was among the sharpest people I have met in my life. A legendary self-mythologizer and bullshitter, he had no appetite for a second-rate performance from the likes of me. He always cut to the chase, old Allen did.

The next phone call involved the Barry Miles biography of Allen, due out later that year. Allen wanted some further changes. The fellow on the other end was not obliging him.

Mistakes had gone uncorrected, Allen insisted. There was still time, Allen insisted. This went on for quite a bit. Allen didn't raise his voice, but he was mildly bullying, there was a hint of threat. The conversation ended unsatisfactorily.

Allen was left agitated and muttering. Can you imagine someone writing a biography about you? Even someone admiring with the best intentions, even someone gullible enough to buy 95 percent of your self-justifying bullshit, even someone intent on producing a hagiography disguised as a biography? What if the author inadvertently told the truth about you here and there? Oh, the horror, the humiliation ... With his appetite for fame, as with so much else, Allen introduced discomfort and distress in his life. He had brought this down on himself.

The phone almost immediately began ringing again. "I'm sorry," Allen said to me, picking up the receiver. He was suddenly very alert, in a way I hadn't witnessed before: all the lights switched on in a most impressive fashion. It was a young man he'd been seeing, a boy, actually, fifteen or sixteen, calling Allen from a pay phone at the Jersey City Medical Center. The kid had slipped away from his parents— while they were all, presumably, visiting a sick relation—and was making this surreptitious love call. Had to talk to Allen, see him, etc. You know the drill.

Allen was beside himself, in a terrible panic. "Yes, yes, but we mustn't talk now, yes, yes, of course, but ..." The call didn't last long, but Allen was really knocked off his pins and set to gibbering. I don't doubt for a moment that the FBI had kept Allen in its sights over the years. He had long been denouncing the government, the military-industrial complex, U.S. foreign policy, corporate America, what have you, all in a rather simplistic but generally accurate fashion. At the same time, he had been championing gay sex, free love, pot-smoking, free speech, free this, free that, long before any of these things were fashionable. In fact, while it was dangerous to do so. Allen had been among the first, and most prominent, to accuse the CIA of being involved in the heroin trade in Indochina, during the Vietnam War and afterward.

No question the FBI kept track of Allen, and may well have tapped his line. But he had a rather elaborate paranoid fantasy about the sort of resources it was devoting to nailing him on a morals charge—presumably sex with a minor. The FBI had been monitoring his every move, every conversation, for over forty years, toying with him, torturing him. The trap could snap shut at any moment. And there he'd be—an American Oscar Wilde, without the drolleries.

I tried to be comforting: The FBI does hound and ruin innocent people. In fact, they do so routinely. But if they had been intent on catching Allen with an underage boy, among other things, surely they would have done so years before. Stupid and inefficient an organization though they are, had they chosen to put Allen out of business, so to speak, he'd be out of business.

But Allen seemed to enjoy indulging himself with his assorted obsessions. I found them rather curious, diverting even, but this was my first time through. In the long term, since his obsessions didn't change or go away, I should think they became tedious. Another of Allen's obsessions that he chose to share in the course of our afternoon was Norman Podhoretz—the right-wing public intellectual and author of several repugnant books, including *Making It*. Apparently they had been having at one another since they were both students at Columbia. Podhoretz had been baiting Allen and his beatnik writer friends for decades, as enemies of decency and normalcy and civilized behavior, etc. Why Allen bothered with this noisome creature, editor of *Commentary* for thirty-five years and apologist for every U.S. government predation at home and abroad, is beyond me, though not at all out of character for Allen. He talks about his obsession with Podhoretz in an interview:

> Good old Norman Podhoretz. If he weren't like a wall I could butt my head against, I wouldn't have anybody to hate. And why hate him? He's part of my world, and he's sort of like the character the Blue Meanie . . . Did I ever really hate him, or was I just sort of fascinated by him? I saw him as a scared personage in my life, in a way; someone whose vision is so opposite from mine that it's provocative and interesting . . .

But it was more than that for Allen. He'd dream of Podhoretz, write letters in his head to him all the time, perhaps even sending a few. He was fascinated with Podhoretz, but maybe not so much as he was fascinated by his obsession with Podhoretz, about which he could go on at great length without any special prompting. Yet carrying on about Podhoretz seemed to soothe Allen, perhaps like an extended version of one of the mantras he liked to chant.

Then the phone rang again. Allen stiffened, anxious that it was the boy, but this time it was his old sidekick Gregory Corso. This was familiar territory but not particularly welcome. Corso needed money, fast, presumably for heroin. He would be by directly.

The buzzer rang not long after and admitted a breathless Corso—thirty-five years older than the *Pull My Daisy* version, grizzled, ravaged, but still very much the same guy, the picture of the street punk turned sixty-something. Corso was in no mood for chitchat. He had "friends" waiting in a car downstairs. He needed money and he needed it quick. Corso and Allen had a brief quarrel in the next room and Allen, like an exasperated, indulgent parent, quickly capitulated and went off to write Corso a check. This was clearly an old routine between them. "Talk to August Kleinzahler here while I take care of this. He's an interesting poet."

I smiled at Corso, trying out my best *friendly, deferential* smile. It's not that I wasn't excited to meet him. I'd walked through not a few cities as a youngster with his book of poems *Gasoline* in my pocket: New Orleans, El Paso, Mexico City, Santa Barbara. I was certainly keener to meet Gregory than I would have been to meet, say, Allen Tate. Or Edith Sitwell. But I'd long ago stopped reading him with any pleasure, and he'd long ago given up writing anything of interest.

Corso looked my way briefly, registered mild contempt, and shouted for Allen to "fucking hurry up." Allen grumbled something from the other room, where he was fastidiously entering the amount of the check into his checkbook and tearing off the check. He walked back into the room with a sigh and a most unconvincing minatory glare.

Corso was gone like he'd received the baton in the last leg of a relay race. No thank-you. No good-bye. Junkies really are so one-dimensional, don't you find?

Allen wasn't terribly put out by any of this. Their interaction was of a familial nature. "Did you and Gregory have a chance to talk?" Allen asked solicitously. "No, not really," I said. The room in which we'd been chatting had grown noticeably darker. Evening was on its way. "You don't have to go just yet, do you?" Allen asked. "Soon," I said. He looked and sounded a bit needy. I think that's when he remembered it was Burroughs's birthday. I haven't a clue what reminded him, but off he went again in a great heat and presently had his friend on the other end of the line, solemnly conveying birthday greetings and promising gifts, an appropriate marking of the occasion, etc.

No sooner had Allen gotten off the phone and returned to chat than it rang again. This time it was a university in Pittsburgh. He was reluctant to go and read there, but allowed his arm to be twisted and finally relented. "I'm trying to cut down on these things," he confessed gloomily. "Why don't you?" I said, in the tone of an affectionate but exasperated cousin, a tone that surprised me. "I can't help it. I can't stop."

Really it was time to go. I'd love to stay, really, but I've got to get back. It's been a gas. No, really. He struck me at that moment as more than just lonely. Of course, it was Sunday, and that depressing transitional part of winter afternoons, a time of day and year that would have been more easily handled in the countryside, or almost anywhere other than the East Village. It distressed me to leave him there by himself looking so unhappy.

Ginsberg called me up several months later in San Francisco and we got together, but it was the social, more public Ginsberg this time, even with only a handful of people around. This was a different Allen, rather manipulative, running operations, connecting this one with that one, all quite well-intentioned but a bit exhausting and irritating. He roped me into attending a Buddhist prayer ceremony in the basement of an AIDS hospice, not what I had in mind. But it was fine. A group of us went out to dinner at a Cuban restaurant. Philip Whalen was along, and he and Ginsberg sparred in the way that old friends sometimes do, none of the blows doing much damage. Whalen was grumpy but enjoying taking the piss out of Allen. We promised to keep in touch.

THOM GUNN

There's only one naked lady left, going to ruin out there in the fog amid the dahlias and lavender, its pink trumpet flowers wilted and in tatters. There used to be a couple of dozen of them blooming in the yard every August. Not much else was out there in the yard doing much of anything, so the ladies made quite a spectacle of themselves, like Rockettes in a dusty frontier town. The neighbor on the third floor got a horticultural bee in his bonnet about seven years ago and dug the girls up, except the one. Of course, they weren't symmetrically arranged and, like some outlandish pink crepe accessory, didn't really go with anything else. But I hated to lose them. Like Paris, they looked their best in gray light.

Thom Gunn brought over a sackful of the bulbs (*Amaryllis belladonna*) I don't recall how many years ago, ten or twelve perhaps. He was always doing things like that. He liked gardening and wanted me to partake more fully of its pleasures. After his teaching obligations of the spring term at Berkeley ended every year, he would apply himself to his own small garden, sheltered and southeast-facing. He seemed to enjoy organizing and cultivating his little patch of wild. And in this, as in most things, his approach was methodical, reasoned, and fastidious, even fussy.

Auden writes somewhere that it's good for a poet to have hobbies like gardening and cooking. This advice struck me as sound, and I commend it to young writers. Thom, who was often compared to Auden on account of being queer, famous, and an English expatriate poet living in America, met Auden at least once. They didn't particularly get along. Thom wasn't at all catty about other poets (well, rarely), but at this late stage in his career Auden in public had become *Auden*. Thom remembered him going on at some length about martinis, what constituted a good one and where the best were to be found. This subject would have been of little or no interest to Thom then.

Thom admired Auden, at least his early poetry, which was a large influence on his own early work. Once, over lunch, he told the story of how Auden had come out here to San Francisco in 1954 and given a series of readings, the proceeds of which were handed over to the fledgling San Francisco State Poetry Center in order to establish a reading series (a recent phenomenon popularized by Dylan Thomas) and archive. Auden stayed with Ruth Witt-Diamant, the Poetry Center's founding director, and, in return for his considerable largesse, asked only that he be delivered to gay bars where he might meet young Jewish American males with blond hair.

Thom Gunn arrived in the Bay Area that same year, following a young American Jewish male with blond hair, Mike Kitay, whom he had met and fallen in love with at Cambridge. Mike had been posted to San Antonio, Texas, to do his service in the U.S. Air Force. Thom took a steamship from England, stayed with Mike's family in New Jersey (who took him to Radio City Music Hall, where he probably saw the Rockettes), then moved on to California and took up studies with Yvor Winters at Stanford, an hour's drive south of San Francisco. He got a great deal from his time with Winters and wrote about it at length in what may be his finest essay, "On a Drying Hill: Yvor Winters."

> He wore glasses and smoked a pipe, and both of these served to mask a face that was not in any case volatile. Pleased or displeased, he was most of the time thoughfully of the same expression; his shabby suit, too, always had the same unpressed demeanor. Almost any photograph taken of him in his last two decades shows accurately what he looked like. It was his voice that was remarkable, though I don't think I noticed it until I started taking his classes. He never played tricks with it, and in fact he habitually used a measured tone in conversation, but it was a voice which an actor would have envied, as you noticed as soon as he started to read poetry aloud. It was deep but capable of great variety in its modulation. It has always struck me that the argument of his essay on the audible reading of poetry is a little weakened by the fact that he could read poetry in what from anybody else would have been a monotone but from him was a controlled resonance, suggesting large emotions barely held in reserve.

Later on, after a not entirely comfortable year in San Antonio with Mike, teaching at the (then) very small Trinity College, Thom settled with him in the Bay Area. They remained together, with variations on the theme, for fifty years.

Thom liked to cook, as Auden also recommends, although almost certainly not on account of that recommendation. He wasn't a greatly gifted cook (he was, after all, an Englishman, and an Englishman of a particular generation), but he was more than passable: his pasta dishes were quite good, and he had a turkey recipe that involved cheesecloth, resulting in an uncommonly moist bird. As with his gardening, he was fastidious, methodical and quietly determined, and a bit fussy: sober, spectacles resting on the tip of his nose, recipe book open at the appropriate page, stirring grimly away, eyes on the clock. I enjoyed many meals at his home. I remember one of my very first dinners there. Thom had asked me beforehand if there was anything I didn't eat. I responded as I always do: eggs, eel, and liver. Thom served me liver and bacon. He wasn't making a point, just absent-minded. Cooking chores were rotated according to a predetermined schedule among the members of his household. Given certain lifestyle-related exigencies this schedule was rather flexible, although negligence was registered and not without disfavor or recrimination.

Although we were good friends for twenty-three years, our friendship reached its apotheosis over the last few years of Thom's life, after his retirement from teaching, in our martini matinées. The word *matinée* has an old-fashioned, low meaning, as an "afternoon tryst," but our martini matinées were only that: martinis at both ends of an afternoon movie. Don't get me wrong, Thom could be irrepressibly affectionate, especially after a couple of drinks. The first time he had me over to his place he sat awfully close to me on his sofa in his tight jeans, sleeveless singlet, and revolting tattoos, plying me with pot and wine. It was a bit of a worry for a moment or two. But I was, finally, not his type. And though he was a remarkably handsome sweetheart of a guy, not to mention a Faber poet, he sure as hell wasn't mine.

So all of that got sorted out from the get-go, and Thom was wonderfully kind to the women in my life, one after the other, and all of them adored him. He was a bit like a dream uncle: rather depraved, but endlessly decent, fun, generous, protective, encouraging, and abusive; cruel even, when he felt it warranted. But this was reserved almost exclusively for literary matters, when I'd written something he disapproved of. My writing has had no greater or more steadfast champion, but if he detected mannerism, slackness, want of real subject matter or its honest treatment, he let me have it with both barrels, sometimes firing below the belt. I didn't like it at the time, but it was a gift, really.

About me personally he seldom took issue. If I said something judgmental about someone, he'd give me a look. I was once walking down the street in Berkeley with another poet, quite famous, a truly reprehensible shit. He doesn't care for me, either. We've just had a rather uncomfortable cup of coffee together, probably at Thom's suggestion, and this signature creep and I begin talking about Thom, a friend of both of ours, and the tenor of the conversation changes because we both love and revere Thom, and the creep starts telling a story the point of which is that Thom is the least judgmental person he's ever known. And I agree, not least because Thom puts up with this asshole. But it's true.

The only time Thom took issue with my extraliterary behavior was when I was having an illicit affair. His objection had nothing to do with sexual infidelity and the institution of marriage—how could it?—but he believed that over the course of such relationships one becomes accustomed to lying, and the habit of lying is detrimental to one's poetry.

Thom liked sex a great deal, sex and literature. He was consumed by both and consumed both in heroic proportions. He did his reading, and writing, in the mornings, and he prowled at night in the bars south of Market Street, an area that was known in the old days as South of the Slot, a bleak area of warehouses, small industry, and manufacturing. Nowadays the area is referred to in the tourist guides as SoMa and is a good deal more upscale and trendy. Had Thom lived another few years and gotten a book together, I think he intended to call it *South of the Slot*.

I know more about Thom's literary enthusiasms than the other, but I know a little about the other. He spoke with unreserved and equal enthusiasm about both. I recall one afternoon when we were off on a reading tour together in Maryland and found ourselves in a mostly empty, rather genteel and expensive seafood restaurant out on the highway. The only other customers were a very elderly married couple, carefully attired in old-people sporty formal, dourly and silently attending to their food. The two, clearly regulars, were an older version of the farm couple straight out of Grant Wood's *American Gothic*, transposed to the mid-Atlantic region. Thom, not at all charmed by the restaurant and oblivious to the elderly couple, after a couple of drinks launched into an extended graphic reprise of some pederastic debacle circa 1970. I was more than a little anxious that the oldsters might overhear his vivid rendering of events and drop dead from coronaries. But their closeness, my discomfort, and the emptiness of the dining room, not to mention the disappointing crab cakes and the prospect of a twenty-dollar cab fare back to the hotel, served only to encourage Thom's volubility, and the wine his volume.

I usually met with him for lunch at a pleasant restaurant

on Cole Street, a three- or four-block walk for both of us. The martini matinées became an extension of these lunches. Apart from gossip, politics, what was doing in our lives, assorted mundanities, we mostly discussed what we were reading. Our lunches were by no means regular, and during the terms Thom was teaching, almost nonexistent. He tended to be cranky and inaccessible then. As with so much else, he was diligent and demanding of himself while lecturing. I often had a day job for seasons on end or was out of town for months at a time. After Thom's retirement we got together on a more regular basis, say once every two or three weeks.

The quality and acuity of his observations would startle me from time to time. If you know someone for a long time, you develop a sense of the way their minds work, their particular funds of knowledge, their intellectual propensities, and so forth. But Thom crossed me up any number of times. "Where the hell did that come from?" I'd think to myself. He wasn't at all a show-off. So many intellectuals, particularly university intellectuals, indulge in pissing contests over how much they've read, quoting at length by heart and so on. No wonder they have no friends off-campus. Thom could more than hold his own if sucked into one or another of these contests, but it wasn't his sport. Apart from the bores and creeps, it was this brinksmanship, along with what Thom used to call, referring to London literary society, "the worst sort of village gossip," that put him off literary gatherings. It was a strong dislike we shared, among many other likes and dislikes.

Thom was vain of his good looks and sexual conquests but not of his poetry and learning. He knew the value of the former and was not falsely modest, a trait he once told me he actively disliked in others.

Englishman that he was, however much he warred with the notion, Thom loved no authors more than Shakespeare and Dickens, and revisited both on pretty nearly an annual basis, usually over the summer, when he had the most time. He liked picking up younger men and doing methamphetamine with them, and enjoyed bringing off a splendid poem of his own devising best of all—as you do if you're in that line of work—but he loved rereading Dickens and Shakespeare in his garden, always finding new bits to marvel over. Not that he didn't stray to the Continent, also like the Englishman he was. He was mad for Stendhal, especially *The Charterhouse of Parma*, also Flaubert's *Sentimental Education*. Baudelaire's *Tableaux parisiens* meant quite as much to him as Donne or Marvell or Keats, all of whom meant a great deal. And at least one summer and fall were devoted to learning Italian, or just enough Italian to get profitably through Dante in the original with the help of a crib. He wasn't big on poetry in translation.

I was a prime benificiary of Thom's perspicacity over the years, but so were thousands of students at Berkeley over his forty years or so of teaching there. I tried to get him to allow me to sit in on his class on "the history of the English lyric" one semester, but he said it would make him uncomfortable. My loss. I can't tell you how many books and authors he put me on to over the years. I could write a book . . . Actually, I did, or we did: an anthology of one hundred American poems. It was bravely commissioned by a trade publisher. (What in the world could they have been thinking?) Thom

initially was chary of the project, worried that our friendship would suffer and that we would have to sift through the
work of this and that celebrated no-talent in order to find a
tolerable selection. But I impressed on him that we could
put in or leave out whomever we bloody well liked. That re-
assured him and we set to it in a leisurely fashion over many,
many months. It went quite smoothly, really. We freely ve-
toed one another's choices, me with theatrical disgust,
Thom with chilly contempt. We included a number of people
who made our skin crawl, but Thom was more disciplined
and fair-minded in this regard than me, besides which, that
wasn't what it was about.

The publisher was horrified when he saw the list. "Where's
Sylvia Plath? We haven't even heard of half these people!"
The usual suspects, or most of them, were on board—
Stevens, Eliot, Crane, Pound, Williams; there was even a
poem of Lowell's—but not with their standard anthology
pieces. About 80 percent of Thom's choices either had Eros
in the title or were directly concerned with the troublesome
deity. Nearly half the poets in the collection were women,
but most of those who were included you've probably never
heard of. It was all terribly shocking.

Thom was a great reader of novels. He disdained short
fiction and didn't read much nonfiction, unless it was Edward Gibbon or Darwin. I am nearly opposite in my tastes,
but we did share our enthusiasms. Thom, for instance,
thought Philip Roth was the cat's meow. I didn't. "Try *The
Counterlife*," Thom said. Which I did, and it dazzled me.

Another time Thom said to me, "I've been reading Isaac
Babel for the first time. He's very important to you, isn't he?

Well, of course he is, he'd have to be." I gave Thom a copy of Charles Nicholl's *The Fruit Palace*, which he loved, likewise *Trainspotting*. Almost anything scatological had great appeal. He also enjoyed the Richard Yates books I shared with him. When I was ill at one point I read through all of Derek Raymond, whom I recommend to anyone with a stubborn bacterial infection. "Oh, yes," Thom said, "he's wonderful, isn't he." Sometimes we came on an author separately that sent us both head over heels. I don't recall who got there first, or how, but at one point we were both roaring through the novels of James Buchan and when we sat down to lunch together could barely contain our enthusiasm, like a couple of teenage girls gushing about a cute new boy at school.

During our final lunch, the Thursday before the Sunday he died, we discussed the anthology ("They'll never do it," Thom said) and J. R. Ackerley, the last among the scores of writers I'd never have found had it not been for Thom. "His writing is close in style to Isherwood's," I said to Thom. "Who was influenced by whom?"

"Oh, Ackerley by Isherwood, certainly," he said. "Ackerley didn't do most of his good writing until later in life, long after he'd been a friend of Isherwood's and an admirer of his writing."

After lunch I dropped Thom off at the cheese shop where he always got his pesto and grated pecorino. He was nothing if not regular in his habits: the tea shop on Haight Street, the Alpha Market for plonk and cuts of meat, the Hole in the Wall for sex.

There wasn't much going on in April in the way of movies, so we were strapped, at least so far as our martini matinée routine. I was headed off for a few weeks. We agreed that surely there would be something worth seeing on my return. Our partings, even if for extended periods of time, were never occasions for much physical display. I don't think that Thom really liked being touched very much unless sexually. Shaking hands seemed to confuse and mildly upset him. I'm not terribly comfortable kissing other males. I think what it came to over the years was, on my part, a rather martial tug and squeeze of his shoulder, followed by a partial hug. That seemed to go down okay, and it went down okay that last time. I don't believe either of us thought it would be the last time.

What I remember, and will remember, most vividly about our friendship was traveling around town with Thom on public transport. Neither of us had cars. We were more often than not heading to a movie, and the prospect and the adventure of getting to the cinema seemed to put Thom in high spirits. To travel with Thom was to participate in an erotic mapping of San Francisco out of the bus window. I was reminded of the early Renaissance maps in which significant sites like the cathedral or castle are wildly out of proportion, or the Mappa Mundi, in which Jerusalem is placed at the center of the world and given space equivalent to its spiritual or political importance, not its actual physical size and geographical situation.

For Thom, the city seemed to exist as a complex of erotic sites, assignations, stews. Heterosexual males, in my experience, are without exception tedious and irritating, not to mention unreliable, on this subject. But Thom, on passing a bar or apartment or street corner (in one memorable instance a phone booth in a rather toney part of town) seemed cheerful and nostalgic in equal measure, and almost always had an amusing or interesting anecdote. If one or two sites or parts of the city defied scale on Thom's map in the way the cathedral and castle did in old maps, they would probably be the Stud and the Hole in the Wall, and his Jerusalem would be South of the Slot.

I don't recall when our martini matinées began, exactly. We would have been early for a movie and found ourselves a bar. I am not ordinarily an afternoon drinker, but when I drink I prefer spirits, and like many other drinkers in middle age I have, for the most part, moved from brown-colored spirits to the less punitive clear. My ordinary drink out these days is a Ketel One martini, up with a twist, very dry.

Thom was a wine drinker, and enjoyed a couple of glasses of plonk over lunch. But he seemed to enjoy doing as I did when we were together at a bar, as well as liking the knowledgable sound of my order. So he, too, had a martini, the same as mine. Martinis, as Auden would attest, pack a wallop. Thom banged back his martini, checked his watch, and, seeing we had all of five minutes left till showtime, ordered a second round.

He tended to be exuberant under the influence of alcohol and quite uninhibited. Even when sober he had an enormous laugh, one that would often turn heads in public places. One time we caught a matinée of *Sexy Beast* and after the movie, and after a couple of post-movie martinis that had become over time part of the ritual, we got caught up in a "you fucking cunt" jag. This continued beyond the movie

theater and bar (the very unprepossessing Hockey Tavern)
to the bus and then, having to change buses, at the bus stop
on Masonic and Geary, where we horrified some perfectly
nice old Chinese people; then on the next bus, filled with
people returning home from work and students from high
school. "You fucking cunt." "Who's a fucking cunt, you
fucking cunt?" and so forth. The spectacle would have been
obnoxious enough if the dickheads involved were fourteen-
year-olds, but in this case one of them was seventy-two
and regarded as one of the most important poets in the English language, and the other dickhead, though a good deal
younger, was not at all young.

Thom's mother killed herself when he was a boy. Any child
would be terribly affected by this, I realize, but I think they
were especially close. After his mother's death, reading and
books became his world; even as an adult he tended to view
the world and people through the filter of literature. It's evident in the poetry. Thom's mother had a good friend named
Thérèse. Although his aunts took him in after the suicide and
looked after him, he sometimes stayed with Thérèse, who
had a son his age. I forget exactly what Thom told me about
her—sophisticated, arty, Jewish, somehow involved with
the theater, a good friend of Peggy Ashcroft. What Thom especially liked about Thérèse was that she treated him as an
adult and confided in him, more so than in her own son. I remember in the last year or two of his life Thom talking about
a great snow in the winter of 1947, a snow such as London had
never seen. It had been an unusually cold winter, a legendary winter. Thom was staying at Thérèse's; it was a week-

end or holiday morning, perhaps even Christmas. When he awoke, the city was covered in white, an amazing spectacle; everything come to a halt, nothing but white. I could tell by Thom's expression while recounting the episode that he was, at that particular moment, having pulled back the curtains on that particular morning so many years before, perfectly happy.

EROS & POETRY

He is the son of Chaos, an egg, and unwrought stone.

He is Ker, a sort of anthropomorphic bacillus with wings, but an Erote, a Ker of Life, instead of the black-winged creature Homer described with big white teeth and long, pointed nails that once tore corpses to pieces and drank the blood, a cannibalistic Harpy.

He is a daimon, halfway between god or spirit force and man.

He is the son of Eilithia or Iris. He is the son of Hermes and Artemis, or Hermes and Aphrodite, or Aphrodite and Zeus, or Ares and Aphrodite.

His insignia are the hare, the rose, the cock, and the goat.

He is the youngest of the gods, or he is the oldest.

His chief antagonist is Anteros, the god of mutual love. His companions are Pothos (longing) and Himeros (desire).

In Alexandrian poetry, where children played an important role in magic and cult, Eros degenerates into a mischievous child playing knucklebones, a kind of dice, with Ganymede.

● ● ●

143

There is a related Greek goddess, Até, who personifies delusion, infatuation, and reckless conduct, thus mischief and evil. Hesiod has her as the daughter of Eris (strife); Homer, as the daughter of Zeus, a very troublesome daughter. She is bewilderment and wild impulse. She walks lightly on the heads of mortals without their knowing it. Behind her trail the Litai ("Prayers"), lame, wrinkled daughters of Zeus who, if summoned, heal the wounds inflicted by Até but bring fresh evil upon the stubborn. Zeus expelled her from Olympus and she fell to the earth in Phrygia on the hill that took the name of the Hill of Error, and the spot where Troy was to be built.

Rarely blind in classical literature and never in classical art, Cupid (Eros) became blind or blindfolded in the late Middle Ages and was associated with Night, Synagogue, Infidelity, Death, and Fortune (*caeca Fortuna*). He was especially associated with Death and Fortune, who were not only blind but also personifications of an active force without sight, hitting out at random.

The fifteenth-century French poet Pierre Michault wrote a poem called "La Danse aux Aveugles" in which Love, Fortune, and Death are the three blind powers that make mankind dance to their wanton imperatives:

> Amour, Fortune et Mort, aveugles et bandés,
> Font danser les humains chacun par accordance.

In India he is Kama, who like Eros was the firstborn of the gods at the creation of the universe, Desire being the primal germ of the universal mind. But he is not the fleshy Cupid of the Romans, instead having a fierce aspect. He is the husband of Rati, goddess of sensual desire. He is Dipaka, "the inflamer"; Gritsa, "the sharp"; Maya, "the deluder"; Mara, "the destroyer"; Ragavrinta, "the stalk of passion"; and Titha, "fire."

Kama carries a sugarcane bow that is stretched by a string of bees. He fires arrows tipped with flowers whose scent announces the sweet, inevitable attack of love. (In a fifteenth-century painting by Cranach, Cupid, holding a beehive and being attacked by bees on his arm, chest, and head, looks up complainingly to Venus, who has struck a rather fetching and uninterested pose, *sprezzatura*, underneath an apple tree.

> As a tiger pouncing
> from behind the branches
> seizes suddenly
> the helpless deer,
> her eyes glancing
> from within her blue sari
> have imprisoned me
> in their gaze.
>
> (Bihārī, from *The Satasaī*, translated from the
> seventeenth-century Hindi by K. P. Bahadur)

Eros is Protorhythmos in Dionysian cults, the first dancer and singer, an Orphic figure who gives impulse and rhythm to the dance of creation. Lucian writes:

> It would seem that dancing came into being at the beginning of all things and was brought to light together with Eros, that ancient one, for we see this primeval dancing clearly set forth in the choral dance of the constellations and in the planets and fixed stars, their interweaving and interchange and orderly harmony.

It is Eros who awakens us to the pulse of poetry and dance, its inexhaustible patterns and transformations.

> Love (Amor, Eros) ... can kindle in the souls of others the poetic fire ... no matter what dull clay we seemed to be before ... It was longing and desire that led Apollo to found the arts of archery, healing and divination—so he too was a scholar in the school of Love. It was thus that the fine arts were founded by the Muses, the smithy by Hephaestus and the loom by Pallas ...
>
> (Agathon's speech in Plato's *Symposium*)

> Things base and vile, holding no quantity,
> Love can transpose to form and dignity.
>
> (Shakespeare, *A Midsummer Night's Dream*)

Christianity turned Eros into the harmless little rubicund fatty of Valentine's cards.

Eros has to do with penetration and then infection. There is quickening of the pulse and cutaneous vasodilation. The face changes expression and takes on an unhealthy pallor, followed by loss of appetite and weight. Lassitude sets in, then reclusiveness.

"Utterly hotheaded and reckless; as a man who would do a somersault into a ring of knives; as one who would jump into a fire," remarks Socrates about a disciple who had just kissed a youth of great beauty.

> Daphnis and Chloe dreamt that the Nymphs—the ones in the cave with the spring in it, where Dryas had found the baby—

were handing Daphnis and Chloe over to a very autocratic
and beautiful small boy who had wings growing out of his
shoulders and carried tiny arrows along with a tiny bow ...
So Daphnis, who was set on fire by all this, used to plunge into
streams ... and often he would actually drink the water in
hope of extinguishing the fire inside him.

(Longus, *Daphnis and Chloe*, translated by Paul Turner)

Dr. J. N. MacKenzie, surgeon to the Baltimore Eye, Ear
and Throat Charity Hospital, asserted in 1884 that the res-
piratory and olfactory mucosa has a structure analogous to
the spongy central body of the penis and is equally erectile.

Only human beings look at one another while making love.

> Youre yën two wol slee me sodeinly:
> I may the beautee of hew nat sustene,
> So woundeth it throughout myn herte keene.
>
> (Chaucer, "Merciless Beauty")

> Wine comes in at the mouth
> And love comes in at the eye;
> That's all we know for truth
> Before we grow old and die.
>
> (Yeats, "A Drinking Song")

> On this feast day, O cursed day and hour,
> Went Hero thorough Sestos, from her tower
> To Venus' temple, where unhappily,
> As after chanced, they did each other spy.
>
> . . . .

And in the midst a silver altar stood;
There Hero sacrificing turtles' blood,
Veiled to the ground, veiling her eyelids close,
And modestly they opened as she rose:
Thence flew love's arrow with the golden head,
And thus Leander was enamored.
Stone still he stood, and evermore he gazed,
Till with the fire that from his countenance blazed,
Relenting Hero's gentle heart was strook:
Such force and virtue hath an amorous look.

(Marlowe, "Hero and Leander")

The sebaceous glands occur all over the body. Their secretions flow into canals in which bacteria break down the odorless sebum into a pungent mix consisting primarily of fatty acids. The rancid, goaty odor of stale sweat is due to these fatty acids.

The apocrine glands in the axillae are responsible for most of a person's body odor. The odor of the axillary organ resembles musk, the perputial sac secretion of the Himalayan musk deer. Apocrine glands are densest in the armpits, the pubic region, and the area around the anus, face, and scalp. The axillary odor consists of a number of musky-smelling steroids. Steroid hormones are produced by the gonads, and their broken-down structures impart to urine its musky odor.

One of the steroids produced in the axillary organ is the same substance that is known to be a mating pheromone in the pig. The odor, which is urinous, is produced in the boar's saliva and when perceived by a sow in heat induces her to adopt the characteristic mating position.

If I kiss Anthea's breast,
There I smell the phoenix nest:
If I her lip, the most sincere
Altar of incense, I smell there.
Hands, and thighs, and legs, are all
Richly aromatical.
Goddess Isis can't transfer
Musks and ambers more from her:
Nor can Juno sweeter be,
When she lies with Jove, than she.

(Herrick, "Love Perfumes All Parts")

Perfumes can be analyzed in their parts: the upper notes
are made from the sexual secretions of flowers, produced to
attract animals for the purpose of cross-pollination and often formulated as mimics of the animal's sex pheromones.
Many of these contain compounds with a fecal odor. The
middle notes are made from resinous materials that have
odors not unlike those of sex steroids, while the base notes
are mammalian sex attractants with a distinctly urinous or
fecal odor (D. Michael Stoddart, *The Scented Ape*).

So quicke, so hot, so mad is thy fond sute . . .

(Campion)

A touch from any part of her had done 't
Her hand, her foot, her very look's a cunt.

(John Wilmot, Earl of Rochester,
"The Imperfect Enjoyment")

How sweet is your love, my sister, my bride!
how much better is your love than wine,

1 4 9

and the fragrance of your oils than any spice!
Your lips distil nectar, my bride;
honey and milk are under your tongue,
the scent of your garments is like the scent of Lebanon.
A garden locked is my sister, my bride!
A garden locked, a fountain sealed.
Your shoots are an orchard of pomegranates
with all choicest fruits,
henna and nard,
nard and saffron, calamus and cinnamon
with all trees of frankincense, myrrh and aloes
with all chief spices.
A garden fountain, a well of living water
and flowing streams from Lebanon.

Awake, O north wind, and come, O south wind!
Blow upon my garden, let its fragrance be wafted abroad.
Let my beloved come to his garden, and eat its choicest fruits.

(The Song of Solomon)

Mina Loy writes in the first of her love songs:

Spawn   of   Fantasies
Silting the appraisable
Pig Cupid   his rosy snout
Rooting erotic garbage
"Once upon a time"
Pulls a weed   white star-topped
Among wild oats   sown in mucous-membrane

I would   an   eye in Bengal light
Eternity in a sky-rocket

Constellations in an ocean
Whose rivers run no fresher
Than a trickle of saliva

There is a trade-off in pain attending all this feasting and rooting unlike anything else. There is great, subterranean shifting and displacement, as if of continents and tectonic plates, as if of one's inner organs. And into the breach pours appetite, an appetite that cannot be slaked.

> . . . love-struck wretches
> Who, on the very verge of consummation,
> Can't make their minds up, thrash about, uncertain
> Which they should pleasure first—their hands? their eyes?
> So they bear down with all their weight, or squeeze,
> Tight as they can, the body they have sought,
> They make it hurt, take hold of lips with teeth,
> Kiss with insistent fierceness. Such delight
> Is never pure, for in its impulse lies
> The appetite for pain, the urge to hurt,
> The germinal seeds of madness. Even so,
> In the very midst of love, ever so lightly,
> Venus abates the punishment, and blends
> A sweetness with the sharpness of the bite.

(Lucretius, *De Rerum Natura*,
translated by Rolfe Humphries)

Eros, The Bittersweet, the title of a book on Eros and poetry by Anne Carson, is from Sappho's *glukupikron*:

Eros once again limb-loosener whirls me
bittersweet, impossible to fight off, creature stealing up.

Eros is something quite specific, as opposed to describing any and all aspects of love and sexuality. It is desire. I realize that the word has become fashionable, thus next to meaningless, but it's the best we've got and it will have to do. It is a desire that cannot be fulfilled without jettisoning the set of tensions that describe the nature of Eros.

> Heard melodies are sweet, but those unheard
>   Are sweeter; therefore, ye soft pipes, play on;
> Not to the sensual ear, but, more endeared,
>   Pipe to the spirit ditties of no tone:
> Fair youth, beneath the trees, thou canst not leave
>   Thy song, nor ever can those trees be bare;
>   Bold lover, never, never canst thou kiss,
> Though winning near the goal—yet, do not grieve;
>   She cannot fade, though thou hast not thy bliss,
>   Forever wilt thou love, and she be fair!

(Keats, "Ode on a Grecian Urn")

Thus, we are compelled to discount what we casually think of as erotic literature, be it the bawdy ballads and catches of Anon. ("A comely Dame of Islington / Has got a leaky Copper; / The Hole that let the liquor run, / Was wanting of a Stopper . . .") or a chill rising through the sleeve of the lovelorn Izumi Shikibu, or Bataille's little Michele dipping her twat in a bowl of milk. Likewise, most of the love conventions and motifs fall outside of Eros's purview, be it Swahili marriage chants or the inadvertently comical posturing and hyperbole of Anne Sexton's "In Celebration of My Uterus" or Charles Bukowski's *Love Is a Dog from Hell.*

• • •

One can only speculate on what caused the erosion and disappearance of the convention of Eros in English. The fashionable love poetry of today reads like Oprah-babble, but with line breaks. Perhaps it had to do with Romanticism and the evolution of the individualistic, psychological "I." There are remnants of the convention here and there, like Edward Arlington Robinson's old Greenwich Villagey curio, *Eros Turranos*.

The convention does exist, and thrive, in contemporary popular music; rock, country, blues, you name it:

Ooooooooeee, baby, you're driving me crazy, etc.

And it endures in fiction. Kawabata's *Snow Country* is erotic. So are *Death in Venice* and *Lolita*. Henry Miller is *not* erotic.

It might be mentioned in this context (given the natures of the adored and the adoring in the three aforementioned titles) that Eros exists independently of procreation or of any Darwinian notions of sustaining or improving the species. Traditionally, erotic poetry involves illicit love, and the objects of this love are often courtesans, servants, the very young, members of the same sex, and those already married. It's trouble.

> Unhappie is the man for evermair
> That tills the sand and sawis in the air;
> But twice unhappier is he, I lairn,
> That feedis in his hairt a mad desire,
> And follows on a woman throu the fire,
> Led by a blin and teachit by a baim.
>
> (Mark Alexander Boyd, "Venus and Cupid")

Forbidden fruit is responsible for many a bad jam.

(country-and-western song)

Lucretius, in the magnificent Book **IV** of his *De Rerum Natura*, does it nicely:

> For normally men fall *toward* a wound, and blood
> Wells outward *toward* the blow that wounded us;
> Yes, if the enemy's close, he's drenched with blood.
> Thus he who's wounded by the bolt of love
> ... turns toward the source of hurt, and aches for union,
> To jet his humors, body into body ...

(translated by Frank O. Copley)

Aristophanes, in Plato's *Symposium*, tells us that originally there were three sexes, one of which partook of the nature of man and woman but has since vanished from the earth. Also, originally each human being was a rounded whole, with double backs and flanks forming a circle. The creature had four hands, four legs, and two identical faces upon a circular neck with a common head, the faces turned in opposite directions. When this creature wanted to run quickly it made use of all eight limbs, turning rapidly over and over in a circle, like a tumbler performing cartwheels. The male sprang from the sun, the female from the earth, and the hermaphrodite from the moon, which partakes of the natures of both sun and earth. These creatures, in their arrogance, finally challenged Zeus's authority and were punished by being cut in two. Thus, each yearned for the other half from which it had been severed. Zeus took pity on

154

them and, with Apollo's help, moved their reproductive organs to the front so the two halves could be rejoined, however temporarily, through intercourse. Again, Lucretius:

> . . . Eagerly
> They press their bodies close, join lips and tongues,
> Their breath comes faster, faster. All in vain,
> For they can gather nothing, they cannot
> Effect real penetration, be absorbed
> Body in body, utterly. They seem
> To want to do just this. God knows they try,
> Cling to each other, lashed in Venus' chains
> Till finally, all passion spent, they die,
> Relaxed completely from that violence,
> Melted, undone; so, for a little time,
> The furious fire subsides. But it will blaze,
> Break out again in madness, and they'll seek
> Again whatever it is they want to reach,
> Find no prescription, no device to stop
> This rank infection, so they peak and pine,
> Confused and troubled by their secret wound.

(translated by Rolfe Humphries)

The interrelationships between Eros and poetry occur on any number of levels. Surely the intensity of the experience, the white heat of desire, drives us out of our atmospheres, quotidian and psychological, and causes us to see. Eros is not the sole transforming emotion that causes us to see, but it's a humdinger. One would not ordinarily choose for himself a passage through anguish, yet poets seem to cultivate it, and at grievous risk. From a sort of actuarial point of view, one cannot pass through these flames too many times without becoming terminally flambéed.

> Love greatly resembles an application of torture or a surgical operation. Do you hear these sighs—preludes to a shameful tragedy—these groans, these screams, these rattling gasps? Who has not uttered them, who has not inexorably wrung them forth? . . . These eyes rolled back like the sleepwalker's, these limbs whose muscles burst and stiffen as though subject to the action of a galvanic battery—such frightful, such curious phenomena are undoubtedly never obtained from even the most extreme cases of intoxication, of delirium, of opium taking. The human face, which Ovid believed fashioned to reflect the stars, speaks here of an insane ferocity, relaxing into a kind of death.

> (Baudelaire, *Intimate Journals*,
> translated by Christopher Isherwood)

The great compendium of love's torments is to be found in Burton's *Anatomy of Melancholy*.

> But the Symptoms of the mind in Lovers are almost infinite, and so diverse, that no Art can comprehend them: though they be merry sometimes, and rapt beyond themselves for joy, yet most part, Love is a plague, a torture, an hell, a *bitter-sweet* passion at last . . . For in a word, the Spanish Inquisition is not comparable to it; a torment and execution it is, as he calls it in the Poet, an unquenchable fire, and what not? From it, saith Austin, arise biting cares, perturbations, passions, sorrows, fears, suspicions, discontents, discords, wars, treacheries, enmities, flattery, cozening, riot, lust, impudence, cruelty, knavery, &c. . . . Every poet is full of such catalogues of Love Symptoms. [my italics]

This section of the book, "Symptoms of Love," goes on for a number of pages until the reader comes, with relief, to "Remedies of Love."

Another source on the subject is Ficino's fifteenth-century commentary on Plato's *Symposium*. Ficino is much taken by blood, choler, and the vapors that attend bestial love, as opposed to divine or human love.

> ... The entire attention of a lover's soul is devoted to continuous thought about the beloved ... Moreover, wherever the continuous attention of the soul is carried, there also fly the spirits, which are the chariots, or instruments of the soul. The spirits are produced in the heart from the thinnest part of the blood. The lover's soul is carried toward the image of the beloved planted in his imagination, and thence toward the beloved himself. To the same place are drawn the lover's spirits. Flying out there, they are continually dissipated.
>
> ... When the pure and clear blood is dissipated, there remains only the impure, thick, dry, and black ... For from dry, thick and black blood is produced melancholy, that is, black bile, which fills the head with its vapors and dries out the brain.
>
> ... When the ancient physicians observed these things, they said that love was a passion very close to the disease of melancholy. And the physician Rhazes taught that it was cured by coitus, fasting, inebriation and walking.
>
> (translated by Sears Jayne)

One modern scholar, J. R. Broadbent, avers that synesthesia and the crowding together of heavy stresses (like the lover's breaths?) serve the specifically erotic poem. He cites two examples:

> There are fragrances, fresh as the flesh of children,
> Sweet as the oboe, green as the prairie.
>
> (Baudelaire, "Correspondences,"
> translated by Kate Flores)

> When all my five and country senses see,
> . . . .
> The whispering ears will watch love drummed away
> Down breeze and shell to a discordant beach,
> And, lashed to syllables, the lynx tongue cry
> That her fond wounds are mended bitterly.
> My nostril see her breath burn like a bush.
>
> (Dylan Thomas)

In her essay "Love's Knowledge," Martha Nussbaum writes about *katalépseis*, about the cataleptic impression having the power, through its own felt quality, to convince us that things could not be otherwise. "But this knowledge, which the shrewdest perceptions of the mind would not have given me, had now been brought to me, hard, glittering, strange, like a crystallized salt, by the abrupt reaction of pain" (Proust, *Remembrance of Things Past*).

Eros awakens us to the world and its particulars and helps us to order experience into artful shapes and rhythms, but by courting the daimon the poet is challenging the gods with all the insolence and overweening ambition of the original humans, only to risk being incinerated or cut in half, one part of himself forever looking in vain for the other.

All things unnatural fly in the face of Hortense's atrocious gestures. Her solitude is the mechanism of love; her lassitude, its dynamic. Under the supervision of children, she has been, in many ages, the burning hygiene of all races. Her door is open to destitution. There, the morality of beings of the present is disembodied in her passion or her actions—O terrible shudder of unpractised loves on the bleeding ground and in transparent hydrogen! find Hortense.

(Rimbaud, "H," translated by Oliver Bernard)

Part Four

CUTTY, ONE ROCK

They didn't look like hoods, more like midcareer bureaucrats, fortyish, chubby, thick glasses. But they'd brought two good-looking molls with them; I can't imagine they were even eighteen: blonds, Marty and Will. It fell to me to keep the boys entertained while my brother retired to his bedroom with the two Mafiosi for what was to be a very, very serious conversation. My brother had warned me that there was a good chance they'd kill him, and, without spelling it out, that if I was on hand my own health might be in jeopardy. We were very close at that stage. I loved my brother more than anyone in the world, and didn't have anywhere else to go.

I wasn't all that much older than the blondie boys: twenty-one. But these were two very silly, giggly kids, and dumb as posts. They didn't find me terribly amusing, either, and made something of a show of it, joking between themselves. But they liked their soda and nuts, so I kept all that going on: my brother was always long on ginger ale and pistachios.

From a distance of more than thirty years, it feels, in the writing, like fiction, hard-boiled fiction some of it. But it isn't, none of it is. My brother would be dead inside six months, but not that night. The three of them were in the bedroom a long time. I had no idea what I'd do if they killed him. I was there to give what's called moral support. I would have said then, and now, that my brother was a nice man through and through, truly decent, and wouldn't hurt anyone on purpose unless they weren't nice or provoked him. But he sure did get himself into some shit.

My brother always had unsavory friends. His nickname in high school was "Gangster," mostly because he was from North Jersey and we had gangster neighbors. "Gangster from Gangsterland," they'd tease him. But he also carried the tag because he was tough and found his way into all kinds of fights when you'd never have guessed there was any fighting to be done.

He wasn't a big man; he was short and square-built. But he was powerful and fast and he learned to get the most out of that body, in the street and wrestling competitively, first in high school, then at college. Once, when he was in high school and hanging around Central Park, he learned of a boy his own age, a bully boy reputed to be the toughest kid in the park, and with a title to boot, something like "King" or "Prince," along those lines. My brother went out of his way to find the boy, who was sitting against a tree surrounded by admirers, and said something provocative to him, and as the kid made ready to stand up, my brother hammered him, snapping the boy's head back against the tree trunk. Fight over. Gangster from Gangsterland.

He was much admired by his peers, for such feats involving recklessness and pluck, but also for his good humor, his sense of fun, and his kindness. It may not seem very kind to insult a stranger, then smack him in the head with all your might, but the other boy was most assuredly not a nice boy and my brother had probably heard ill of him somewhere along the line.

Also, he was clever. He knew that if the other boy managed to get up and make it a fair fight, the result might well be different. It was a calculated gamble. A dangerous gamble. Above and beyond anything else, my brother was a gambler. A professional gambler until his death at twenty-seven. Poker. High-low was his action. He was a major leaguer in that line, and regrettably there's a formidable attrition rate as regards high stakes and its lifestyle equivalent.

But it was high stakes from the start with my brother: forty-eight- or seventy-two-hour marathons with thousands of dollars changing hands, all before he was twenty. He played a lot of poker during his time at the Wharton School in Philadelphia during the early sixties: he usually played with an older crowd that included Sonny Liston's and Joey Giardello's handlers and associates. How a nineteen-year-old at Wharton wound up playing with these thugs is beyond me, but my brother never lied about these things. If anything, he soft-pedaled his more outré associations or simply neglected to mention them.

He did manage to get his degree. Also, he escaped Philadelphia without being killed or killing anyone else, a narrow escape on both fronts. On one occasion he threw some big palooka who was beating up his girlfriend through the plate-glass window of a shop. Then the girl came after my brother; and then the palooka, shaking the glass off. But my brother was a speedy guy, too. Another time, he somehow got into it with several greasers late one night at a restaurant-dive. He took care of a couple of them, but the third one got behind him and cracked him on the noggin with a piece of crockery. I forget how he got out of that one without a knife in his back, but he did find himself struggling with his statistics homework for a while.

Another time, when he was home from college on a spring or winter break, he called my father from a White Castle hamburger joint and told the old man he'd got himself into a situation with a dozen or so greasers and could my father maybe drive over and rescue him. Of course, my father loved shit like this and dragged me along, age fourteen or so. Well, we get there and it's looking pretty tense inside the restaurant. North Bergen certainly had, and probably still has, its rough edges. So my father starts honking his horn and making violent hand gestures, sticking his finger in his teeth, flashing the V sign, the cuckold sign, bouncing up and down in the driver's seat, looking like a crazy person. As the greasers took in this spectacle, pie-eyed and with some concern, my brother made his exit. On the drive home, my father gave forth with some extreme editorializing about my brother's predisposition to trouble. But the old man got a thrill out of it. He and my brother had their problems, not least because they resembled each other in their belligerent behavior, but they loved each other even more on account of it, I think.

It could get a bit primal around the house before my brother eventually left for college in order to devote himself full-time to trouble. The difference between them when they'd go off was that my father had an unmanageable temper and my brother, when he was fighting, was very cool. By the time he was sixteen he was already a champion wrestler and seasoned street fighter, and could handle my father pretty well. Oh, the old man would knee him in the balls and pull all manner of Jersey City stunts, but my brother would prevail and not take it out too badly on the old man.

My brother was not only tough and self-destructive, he was handsome. He was fit as hell—hundreds of push-ups and the rest—and he had a good-looking mug: good bones, a nicely shaped head, a straight nose, brown eyes, a full mouth. A bit like the young Marlon Brando, in fact, especially around the eyes. In this good fortune, he took after the men on my mother's side of the family. Me, I got stuck with the other.

In retrospect, for someone that good-looking and wild, he didn't have a lot of girlfriends at school. Yes, he got into trouble when he was fifteen or so when my folks found out that he and a buddy had been visiting whores in some bad neighborhood or other. But I suspect he liked the ambience and proximity of danger. He was also experimenting with heroin around this time, and not much later found some of those very early LSD-laced sugar cubes. Quite the pioneer, my big brother. But there weren't that many girls.

He was a great brother, if somewhat elusive: busy breaking noses, hitting home runs, building model airplanes, racing in the soapbox derby. Sometimes, when he was older and going into the city all the time, I'd climb into his bed and wait up until he got home. I remember the smell of his pillow. When he finally arrived I'd badger him with questions until he'd chase me back to my room. Then, if I was lucky, he'd play *tap-tap* with me, a sort of Morse code game on the common wall between our rooms, until he got bored.

He never hit me in anger, though he hit me plenty. Our relationship was physical from the time I was big enough for roughhousing. I did get hurt pretty often, but he didn't do it on purpose: six and a half years older, he was simply bigger and stronger.

Verbally, too. When I was seven or eight he told me I was obnoxious. He'd called me all sorts of synonyms for "obnoxious" in the past, but this, for some reason, was devastating. I even remember where we were, what room. I didn't know the meaning, but I knew what he meant. It was such a grown-up word. It was as if he'd punched me in the stomach. That was the moment at which I resolved to become a man of letters. If there were words that could be as punishing as this, I wanted my quiver to be full of them. As with the physical roughhousing, he never played to wound. And he had affectionate names for me, too: one was "lover boy." He was physically affectionate as well. He'd always give me a kiss, even if it was after bloodying my nose.

We engaged in all sorts of games and contests, but until I was grown-up enough to give him some competition, it must have been frustrating for him. We'd make bets: whoever lost would have to tickle the other's back, the wager being in minutes of back tickling. I'd usually lose big-time, but he paid up when he had to. I was never particularly thrilled at having to tickle his back for thirty minutes, but it was one way of being close to him and his not growing bored and running off after five or ten minutes.

One summer I grew up, filled out. My brother, who by that time had graduated from college and was working as a financial analyst for a New York firm, was at the house in Jersey, visiting. It was summer. We were eating dinner out on the porch and he was checking me out, appraising my arms and shoulders. "I think we need to get hold of some boxing gloves," he announced. Of all the things on earth that my family didn't need, it was boxing gloves. No one in that household needed that sort of encouragement. My father, naturally, thought it was a perfect idea. My mother, quite sensibly, asked why we needed them, but it was a rhetorical question and delivered in a resigned tone of voice.

The gloves arrived not long afterward. It was warm still, a couple of hours until dark. After dinner my brother and I had our gloves laced up by what struck me as an overeager father. I wasn't especially keen, quite the contrary. As my parents sat watching from the screened-in porch, finishing their dessert, my brother and I marched down the back stairs and into the yard—the after-dinner entertainment.

It started well enough: I was in good shape then, sixteen or seventeen, a wrestler like my brother with a similar build, but nowhere close to what he had been in his prime. His deterioration had already begun, from the cigarettes and drink, the late nights, the desk job, the irregular life. We touched gloves and went at it. My butterflies (which had been more like chrome-plated bats) vanished. I've always enjoyed that about sport and fighting: the moment when the adrenaline kicks in. We were jabbing a bit, feeling each other out, and then we began mixing it up. I had him on his heels, banging away as much out of fear as anything else; as long as I was hitting him, he wasn't hitting me. And then I nailed him with a left hook, a shot that stunned him and knocked him back a step. I waded in, emboldened, to see what further damage I could do.

The next thing I remember is my mother standing over me, screaming, "What did you do to your brother?" while my father, with a jovial smirk, checked my brother's split lip. "Look what you've done to your brother!" my mother hollered. "How can he go to work on Monday looking like that?" My brother looked down at me, most amused at my being reprimanded while prostrate and semiconscious. Of the three of them he was the one most likely to have given me a hand up, but he was entangled in my mother's frantic ministrations.

My brother had been living in the city for five years or so when he told me he was queer. He'd lived first in the London Terrace complex in Chelsea, then down at the bottom of the West Village, on Charlton Street off Sixth Avenue. Over the years, I'd visit him and we'd get high, go out to dinner, goof around. It was always a thrill for me, a season's highlight. He knew how to have fun, like a big kid with a fat wallet: a sweet, dangerous, hedonistic delinquent.

It would have been 1970—the fall, I think. A transitional time of year, at any rate. I had dropped out of college and had been knocking around the continent pretending I was Jack Kerouac. My folks weren't too thrilled with me, so when I came to town I stayed in the Village with my brother. He had begun to take more of an interest in me now that I showed signs of developing into a full-fledged fuckup.

I remember the particular day and evening because I'd visited his doctor to be looked after for a venereal complaint, and he went along, too, to have a vitamin B_{12} injection, like JFK used to get. He had a cold and said he had a large evening planned, which, to my surprise, involved me.

The program that evening was to drop some acid and go out, see what the night might hold in store. We'd gone this route before. You can imagine what fun it was tripping with someone like my brother: I mean, on top of everything else, money was never any object (no matter how deep his gambling debts), and he knew all manner of charming sociopaths who couldn't be nice enough to his baby brother.

When we dropped acid my brother liked to smoke a little weed first, and as the initial LSD rush was coming on, to enjoy a jolt of amyl nitrate. Well, now, that was blasting off in style. The only downside was my brother's taste in music: he'd insist on listening to Pink Floyd as these Mission-to-Control sessions came to a climax. I had my own ideas about an appropriate soundtrack, but he was the master of ceremonies, no questions asked.

It was a nice apartment, comfortable, a one-bedroom facing onto the street. He liked nice things: a teak coffee table, carvings, captain's chairs, a great big maroon couch (where I crashed), long bookshelves packed mostly with science fiction—he figured *Dune* and *Stranger in a Strange Land* were the cat's cuffs, real works of genius. I remember when he was a teenager he'd become infatuated with certain books: *Look Homeward, Angel*, Nigel Dennis's *Cards of Identity*, *Steppenwolf*, *The Dwarf* by Pär Lagerkvist, *A Separate*

Peace. He'd be in a trance for days. He wrote poetry, too, well into his college years, maybe a year or two after: violent, dark stuff, stripped down, not much in the way of figurative language or fancy stepping. I suppose it wasn't very good; in fact, I know it wasn't. But I identify it with him so regard it as sui generis.

I imitated everything about my brother, down to his eccentric handwriting and way of holding a whiskey glass, mannerisms of his which, along with scores of others, have become my own. I often think that we're all mere composites of our favorite people's habits: the way we talk and gesture and laugh, how we comb our hair and walk. I'd dutifully read most of the books he found so wonderful and enjoyed them in varying degrees, but our tastes, as with music, tended to differ, especially as I grew up. I'd kid him about the sci-fi and Pink Floyd, and in response he'd make a great show of his pity for my obtuseness and callow snobbery.

It was chilly out, I remember that; the clocks had probably already been turned back. It was dark. He surprised me when he said, "Let's stop here a minute. I want to talk to you." (There was a little public space on Sixth Avenue, around the corner from his apartment.) He was never one for stopping, even at red lights. And talk to me? Something was up, and off.

Keep in mind that the acid is coming on gangbusters at this point. So he asks me where did I think he went most nights; wasn't I curious? True, he was vague about his comings and goings. I suppose I was a little hurt and confused to be left out of his life as much as I was. But I was so much younger: I idolized him and didn't really feel worthy of his confidence, of being taken as an equal, a pal. He moved in a glamorous orbit of his own wild devising, an orbit in which I didn't belong.

I shrugged and mumbled something. It was cold sitting there on a stone bench. The acid didn't make it any warmer. Something funny was going on; he was different. He was also struggling. He wasn't the type to struggle, or at least to show it. I was finding it all a little overwhelming when, very agitated now, he said to me: "I'm a fairy. I'm queer. I'm a faggot." He said the last with particular revulsion. He was shaking. I couldn't remember him like this before. We'd grown up in an emotionally precarious household and I'd seen him distraught, but nothing like this. This was something else.

Given what was happening with the drug shrieking weird arias in my body and brain, this "faggot" business seemed only another component of a larger event. But part of me, somewhere in there, understood the gravity of the moment, at least as it manifested itself at my brother's end. He had probably been struggling with this for weeks. In retrospect, it must have been one of the most difficult moments in his life, up to that point a double life. No other straight person knew his secret. Not one. And here he was, sharing it with his only brother, who worshipped him, imitated him as best he could. He must have been terrified I would be disgusted and reject him. I doubt he'd have blamed me.

Well, there wasn't much chance of that. I had no real experience of homosexuality apart from the occasional teacher skulking around the gym for no good reason or an effeminate classmate or two. I'd looked through books like

John Rechy's *City of Night* that my brother had lying around. It was mostly about low-life, pathetic guys jerking each other off in Times Square movie houses, near as I could tell. If my brother was queer, I thought, there was no doubt a lot more to it than that.

It upset me to see him so upset. I told him I loved him and that I didn't mind one bit that he was homosexual, which I didn't. It would never have occurred to me, or probably to anyone else, that he was, but frankly, he could have told me he ate a baby for brunch on alternate Sundays and I wouldn't have given a damn. I just wanted to be around him, like always.

A year later I found myself retracing the steps we took that first evening, going from bar to bar. I almost certainly knew that it was too late, but maybe there was an off chance I'd bump into someone who'd seen him.

His evenings customarily began at a bar called Julius's, near Sheridan Square. It seemed a lively place, slightly up-market, Ivy League casual. The only odd bit was that there were no women and a disproportionate number of the men were uncommonly good-looking, like the models you see in catalogs for men's clothing. It was bright in there, noisy, the jukebox playing some of-the-moment dance hit, and from the back an irresistible smell of hamburgers grilling.

It was a merry, friendly atmosphere. We ordered drinks. My brother always ordered "Cutty, one rock." Then he introduced me to his friends, of whom he seemed to have many; all of them teased him about trying to pass off his latest trick as his brother. A couple already seemed aware of my existence, which I found flattering. To a one they checked me out, up and down. But it was a bluff sort of lechery, all in good fun. Julius's provided the overture, the launching pad for my brother's evenings. He'd have a couple of drinks, or three, or four, catch up with his friends, survey the talent on hand, and after an hour or so head west, usually to the International Stud.

He spent a lot of time at the Stud, so much so that the owner, who looked a religious type, with his beard and black fedora, turned up at his funeral, praying like mad in a big voice that drowned out the others. My brother would have a lot of Cutty, one rock, at the Stud. And he fed an awful lot of quarters into the pool table. But the owner probably just liked my brother. There wasn't much good to be found in actively disliking him, though I don't recall him picking too many fights in gay bars. A scowl or two, maybe an invitation to step out on the sidewalk, but that's all.

The Stud was more crowded and noisier than Julius's. The music was louder; it wasn't a conversation spot. The boys here were more serious about cutting to the chase; my brother, too. I remember a pair of young blond twins, acquaintances of his, cornering me on one of my first visits and showing me their new tits. These were very girly boys and they were clearly giving me the business, aware that I was straight but also well aware that they were cute enough, post–hormone shots, to give a straight guy serious pause. But mostly I amused myself at the pool table. One time my brother introduced me to a "famous English poet," a tall, handsome-looking galoot in a T-shirt and leather vest, with lurid tattoos on his arms. He didn't look like any sort of poet to me, more like a predatory sex addict. Had someone told me then that he would become one of my dearest friends, I would have laughed in disbelief.

At this point in the evening my brother would begin wandering back and forth between the Stud and a place called Danny's, a quieter venue, not really a dive, although you wouldn't want to take your aunt Grace there. It was at Danny's that my brother would hook up with some of his gambling and underworld associates. I remember him asking the bartender if he'd seen so-and-so. I don't think sex had anything to do with it. Money did.

There was also a little coffee shop my brother would hit late at night, a last-chance spot for tricks. It wasn't much of a place, certainly no place we could hang out. But he seemed to have a fair bit of luck there before he'd call it a night. A more congenial cruising ground, at least in milder weather, was along Christopher Street. I enjoyed sitting with him on the stoops and taking in the world while he was taking in the talent. One time we were sitting there, probably around midnight, and two straight guys walked by, probably Jersey boys, and muttered something about faggots. They were looking at us. Big brother didn't care for that one bit . . .

Now, it might seem odd, perhaps unsalubrious, that I should be tagging along with my older brother as he chased after younger men. But it was fun. My brother was fun. And what did I do when my brother found himself a trick to take back to his apartment? I'd get lost for two or three hours, probably somewhere east of Sixth Avenue, in the vicinity of Washington Square, at a more sedate watering hole, with more wood than chrome and a jukebox inclining more toward jazz and smoky-voiced balladeers than toward disco, where I might come across the occasional young lady.

Not long after my brother unburdened himself to me, I wound up living with him for extended periods, setting up camp on the couch where we had smoked so many joints and eaten so many pistachio nuts. Of course I was delighted by the arrangement. To my surprise, so was he.

What always intrigued me about the night world he inhabited was that, unlike the straight pickup scene, the gay scene was a seven-night-a-week affair. True, Sundays and Mondays were a tad quiet, but this crowd seemed to be as indefatigable as they were incorrigible. While the rest of America slept, NORAD and these guys were on constant alert. Yet every morning my brother would get up early, put on his J. Press suit, rep tie, and brogues, and head off to work. And every evening he would come home, light a joint, think about dinner, then head off up Sixth Avenue, "west with the night."

It wasn't only to Julius's, Danny's, and the Stud. My brother, who had a pathological aversion to boredom, was never against improvisation. He always had his secondary, tertiary, and come-what-may partying strategies. Nor was he averse to visiting straight clubs if they offered any chance of extreme behavior. Wherever we went, it seemed that we enjoyed privileged entrée. My brother always knew someone: the owner, the maître d', the bartender, the bouncer. "And this is my little brother," he would say proudly, and I was allowed to follow.

He moved in a variety of circles, none of them, apart from his day job, particularly mainstream or wholesome. Figuring large were his gambling cronies, some gay, some straight, the high-stakes poker crowd and the bookies he bet ball games against and the loan-shark hoods who patrolled these waters. I once saw a movie called *The Gambler*, starring James Caan as a self-destructive university lecturer addicted to gambling. The protagonist has a fair bit of my brother in him, enough that when I walked out of the movie theater in 1974, three years after my brother's death, I was shaken.

Someone once suggested to him that he check out Gamblers Anonymous. But he'd have to put that one on the list with Alcoholics Anonymous, Drugs Anonymous, Sex Anonymous, Fighting Anonymous, and Bad Boy Anonymous. There were no twelve-step programs in those days, nor did the terms "dysfunction" and "denial" exist. My brother and I were certainly familiar with the concepts, but pop psychology had not yet found its way into the American mainstream, blessedly. He did, on at least a couple of occasions, give it a go with a psychiatrist, but this never lasted very long. It's not as if he didn't understand that much of his behavior was driven by desperation and self-hate; he wasn't shallow or unreflective, quite the contrary. It was simply the way he was. He was born wild, born troubled. He wasn't designed for the long haul; not everyone is.

●　●　●

For reasons of his own he chose to acquaint me with the wider spectrum of men at play. We visited the parked trucks down by the river under the West Side Highway, which served, late at night, as ad hoc motel rooms. He took me to a club that occupied two floors of a commercial building down by the river. There was a sullen guy at the entrance to check you were okay, then you took a freight elevator up to one of two floors: one floor for dancing and making new friends; the other serving a similar function but with a large back room, a crowded, very public arena, for those who had really hit it off. At one point my brother lifted me onto his shoulders so that I might have a better look at the action. This may have seemed odd, but no odder than the amorous free-for-all that was being played out in front of me under a cloud of cigarette smoke, sweat, and aftershave. We also went a little farther uptown, maybe to Twelfth or Thirteenth, to visit a leather bar or two. There were some dangerous-looking guys there, not just fatties. The two of us would have stuck out in our civvies, and my brother would have reveled in that and in any attendant menace it brought our way. It all struck me as sexual theater: however brutal the interaction, the suffering party seemed more than complicit.

I was pleased to be out of there, but not ungrateful for the education—for a twenty-year-old who was aiming to be a writer and thirsty for experience, it was a lot more interesting than a writing class. My brother, for his part, wasn't trying to sell me the gay life. He loathed the fact of his own homosexuality and was hounded by it to the end. He also kept a close watch on me in case I was lured into something. But there was little chance of that: on the one hand, I was too inhibited; on the other, I was already terminally cunt-struck. I think he was merely trying to broaden my horizons. Expose me to some of the breadth of human behavior. But also, I guess, to share his life with me, with someone he loved and could trust.

Unlike me, however, my brother did experiment, and on more than one occasion tried to get something going with a girl. I'm sure he was as attractive to women as he was to men. He may have struck the conventional gal as a bit crazed, but quite a few women go for that. There was nothing gay in his manner; he was a tough guy, a jock. It's just that he preferred having sex with guys. But, as I said, he did experiment. One experiment was with a pretty lesbian masseuse named LouAnne, who lived with him for a while: dark, curly hair, my age. She spent her work hours jerking guys off at some club uptown. I think he found her in a lesbian bar. Maybe he was looking for a fight: I don't know why else he'd be in a lesbian bar.

One time I came through town when LouAnne was living with my brother. I don't know what had gone on sexually between them, if anything, but she was sleeping on the sofa, not in the bedroom. I took up residence on the floor, in a sleeping bag. I forget the dynamics but we turned out having a go. I'm not sure what was in her head; maybe she felt some kind of obligation to service the straight kid brother. Anyhow, it wasn't much of a go. She certainly was a beautiful girl, if inert, and I was intimidated by her beauty. Afterward, she suggested that I get myself fucked in the ass so that I could appreciate how she felt about having intercourse with me. Sweet, eh? Actually, she was. Sweet. A nasty mouth, but sweet. I was besotted, putting all good sense far behind me, then humming loudly so that it might disappear. My crush inspired only bewilderment and contempt on her part.

I wasn't thinking of my brother when I had at her. I wasn't thinking of much at all. Until I told him about the episode not long afterward. It hurt him, I could immediately see it in his face. I don't think he was in love with her, but they had a friendship of some kind and I think he held out the prospect of something romantic developing. They were both dead solid queer, or so it seemed to me then, and now. Maybe she's a round, genial granny in Sheepshead Bay with gray curls, I don't know. I do know he was desperately trying to straighten out and probably hoping LouAnne would be the girl to help him. I don't suppose he thought I was stealing her; after all, they weren't making it at the time, if they ever had. But I think he would have liked to. Then his piggy little brother mucked things up.

The gambling continued apace, especially the poker. At this point he was playing with some fancy characters, some of them professional. Even I recognized a name or two, and I have no interest in cards. Self-destructive though he was, my brother never set out to lose: not in a fight, where he never lost, and not at the card table, where he sometimes did. He knew betting on football and basketball was a mug's game, but at poker, high-low, he was seriously accomplished.

The problem was, he was forever in debt. Large sums changed hands. Sometimes he'd be up seven or eight thousand when he won, which was often, but he had difficulty collecting, so when he lost he'd wind up having to borrow. He was borrowing from Mob loan sharks.

I used to be able to rattle off the price schedule for assorted Mafia services: retrieving a loan, buying a judge, a contract killing. A hit was alarmingly inexpensive. If you had enough money, you could buy your way out of first-degree murder. These guys owned everybody. You've seen the movies: you don't want to be owing the Mob boys. My brother had a good job, but that didn't begin to cover it. Also, he was a free spender: he liked clothes and the good life, he picked up tabs.

He hung on at his day job. It says something about his discipline and perseverance that he lasted so long while hating it so much. I realize a lot of people hate their jobs, but not too many of them would have been getting whipsawed like my brother between his days and nights. These were big nights for a working stiff, late nights full of too much Cutty, too much pot, too many Marlboros, too many loveless tricks. Then there were the marathon poker sessions, the frantic leveraging of debts. In between there were the fights, car wrecks, broken bones. He started breaking bones quite young. He broke a leg, an arm, a hip, his nose. His knuckles didn't look so good by the end, either.

One time he succeeded in getting the outfit he worked for to send him to San Francisco for a month or two. He was hoping he might take to the place, get clear of New York and all of the assorted messes he'd got himself into. But he didn't care for it. He complained that everybody spent their time and energy talking about how they could never live anywhere else on account of how it was so wonderful in San Francisco.

Naturally, the first thing he did on his way into San Francisco from the airport was to tell the driver to take him to the roughest bar in town; he wanted to see what sort of trouble he could find on the West Coast. The driver probably took him to the waterfront south of Market somewhere; doubtless the place is all yupped up now. Anyhow, he found himself a pool game—and his Cutty, one rock—and lost. He told me later he had the distinct impression that if he'd won he wouldn't have walked out of there alive. As I said earlier, my brother was not given to hyperbole. But he lost. He didn't try to lose. He was just lucky.

We hooked up in Mexico one time. I'd been in Mexico City and the plan was for us to meet up in Acapulco, where he'd booked us a couple of hotel rooms. It was fun. At night we'd drive to the red-light district, each going our separate ways, then meeting up later. At the end of the evening we'd grab a cab up into the hills, way up, to a fancy gay bar called the Sans Souci. It's a famous spot, I think: very pretty, with a view of the city lights, the ocean stretching away into the darkness, the stars glimmering above. It was a large outdoor affair under an impressive thatch. One night I saw my brother making out with a cute young Mexican kid. That unsettled me. I'd never actually seen him making out with a guy before.

One of his moneymaking schemes from this period involved going down to Mexico and sending home a few kilos. The first attempt didn't go very well: some local con artist drove him out in the middle of nowhere and pulled a knife.

Poor man. My brother wasn't sure if he killed him but said the Mexican was lying there very, very still for an awfully long time and turning blue after my brother had whacked him repeatedly in the head with a large rock.

Eventually he found someone he regarded as reasonably trustworthy to sell him a few kilos, which he had carefully packed and shipped, air freight, to Kennedy Airport, where he would pick it up. Regrettably, something seems to have gone wrong. He found himself amid a jovial band of the constabulary at the freight terminal. A felony conviction with probation.

Our parents got wind of that one, all right. I think my father may have had to show up in court. He wouldn't have liked that one bit. Relations were none too good even before that. I don't really blame the folks. They were always having to bail him out, figuratively and literally. He would borrow my father's car and total it on the West Side Highway. He was always hitting my father for money or trying to get him to cosign on a loan. By then my parents took it for granted that he was in trouble of one kind or another, and if he wasn't at that particular moment, he soon would be. But they liked the fact that he put on a nice suit and tie every morning and went to a good job. Something they could tell their friends. About the rest, they didn't want to know.

He didn't always make that easy. I remember him turning up at their house one Sunday evening on acid with a couple of the nelliest faggots you could imagine. They were all a wee bit drunk and noisy on top of the rest. No reaction from Mom and Dad. Mom just wheels out the tea wagon with snacks. Dad, with hearty bonhomie, mixes them a drink. Years after my brother was dead I'd try to tell them he was gay, but they would both simply look at me, blink, and pretend either that they hadn't heard me or that I was a gibbering idiot.

But it was my father who wound up finding him that morning. It was supposed to have been me. My brother had left me instructions, and the key was waiting for me under the mat. But I didn't get the letter until it was too late. I don't relish the thought of walking into that apartment and finding him there on the sofa three days dead and sitting in his own shit. But he'd done plenty for me, and however bad he felt about it, the job was my responsibility. Neither of us would have wanted my father to find him like that. Our relationships with the old man may have been difficult, but we would rather have spared him that.

It was my fault, really. Not that he killed himself. He was going to do that, regardless. It would have been late November. I had a ticket to JFK from Vancouver. I knew what was about to go down. Maybe I thought I could stop him. I don't know. You can't stop people like him. Soon as I'd gone back to school he'd have done it, almost certainly.

But I didn't catch that flight. My girlfriend had phoned up in tears the night before. She was sure she was pregnant. I didn't really believe her. She said she'd got hold of a car and there was a cabin that belonged to a friend, up at Shawnigan Lake. She wanted me to go up there with her, hold her hand. She wasn't pregnant, just a little late, a little needy. A nice girl; well, not all that nice: the estranged wife of a professional hockey goalie whose violent behavior had resulted in his being dispatched to a farm team in the hockey wilderness

—North Carolina, I think it was—where he could spear and maim and concuss to his heart's content and get it out of his system.

So I didn't make that flight. And it was another couple of weeks before I managed to find the money for another one: December 8, 1971, two days before my twenty-second birthday.

My brother had fallen in love during his senior year at college. At the time it seemed only that he was unduly concerned about the psychological condition of a younger friend who had attempted suicide. I can't remember the boy's name or what became of him. My brother was changed by this experience. I don't know what happened between the two of them, but something was altered in my brother. The relationship ended once he moved to New York and began working. I don't know if he figured out he was gay during that last year of school, but he seems to have made up his mind by the time he moved to the city.

It must have been terrifying and exhilarating at the same time: the acceptance of his "pathological" sexuality on the one hand, and on the other the boundless sexual opportunities available to a great-looking, engaging kid freshly moved to New York. Not to mention all the poker games and fights and general trouble a great metropolis could throw his way. He had a good job, money to burn—no wonder the family didn't see much of him those first couple of years. And when he did visit, he was always in a hurry to get back across the river.

My heart used to sink when he'd run off like that after

dinner. It was bad enough when he went off to college for four years, but now, when he was close by, I didn't see much more of him, maybe less. I longed to go back with him to the city, share somehow in that exciting life of his, instead of being stuck at home in Jersey with the folks, wretchedly slogging through high school. But he did seem glad to see me and was always affectionate, if not entirely present. He would have been running very hard in those first few years out of college. He must have been on fire.

One time he was visiting—I think he was still at college—and we were hanging out, teasing each other, good-natured stuff. For no particular reason, I said something like, "I know about your secret." I meant nothing by it, it was a game. But he became very agitated. His voice was wrong. He pressed it: What, exactly, did I know? At first I maintained the tease, coyly refusing to tell him. But he started to get seriously upset, and when I told him I was just kidding, he didn't believe me. He began shoving me around, twisting my arm and the rest, our customary roughhousing. But this time he was meaner, out of character, a little desperate. For all his violent behavior, he had almost no mean in him, especially toward me, but that afternoon was different. He let it all go, finally, but something had gone down that I didn't begin to understand.

In the spring of 1971 I came to town without much going on: still out of school, out of work, out of money. As usual, I took up residence on my brother's sofa. As usual, he seemed glad to have me around and to drag me along with him most evenings as he made his rounds of the bars.

Enjoying bars as much as I had come to do, I considered a career in that area, on the working side of the bar, and enrolled at the International School of Bartending, about eight floors above West Twenty-third Street. The milieu and "professors" were somewhere between Preston Sturges and Damon Runyon, my fellow neophytes not the best and brightest. For two weeks I shook and stirred colored liquids, exhibiting competence at the Singapore Sling but stumbling miserably in my attempts at the Ramos Fizz. The prospect of another four weeks of simulated cocktails began to get me down, likewise the job opportunities: the school, apparently, had an inside track with a chain of surf-and-turf establishments in Schenectady. As I had done with the university and on too many other occasions, I dropped out.

My brother, meanwhile, was planning a significant crime, a state-of-the-art white-collar crime that would liberate him from his desk job forever. By this time, he'd been working as a financial analyst for six years or so. From the beginning, he'd hated it. But it paid, and he needed money to play. The crime was to involve the computers at work and had something to do with siphoning off funds to a dummy corporation. Computer technology wouldn't have been terribly far along in 1971; in fact, it was only that year that the prototype for the microprocessor first appeared. I shouldn't imagine there had been much in the way of sophisticated computer crime.

I don't remember the details, and even if my brother had explained it to me it would have gone in one ear and out the other. He was always good with figures; I am hopeless. I know it involved another guy who worked for the same company, but down in Baltimore: a straight guy with a family. How and when the two hooked up and conspired, I couldn't say. I do remember my brother was delighted with the project. "Absolutely foolproof," he told me repeatedly.

It was good to see him so cheerful and excited: Gangster from Gangsterland. Really, he should have been a full-time criminal; it's one of the few careers that might have sustained his interest. In an earlier century he might have been a gunslinger. He liked Westerns. He liked the notion of the outlaw—not the mean outlaw who is rude to the saloon lady, but the Robin Hood kind: the outsider, the existential hero, the lone wolf, the fellow who stares death in the face and doesn't blink, that sort of thing. Poker fulfilled that role for him, I think. Check out *The Cincinnati Kid* sometime. My brother liked that one. He liked the book better, but he liked the Steve McQueen character in the film, the gambler, the five-card-stud player, the kid who comes to town to take on the Man (Edward G. Robinson). My brother liked the notion of being the kid, the hard-living, hard-loving, haunted, hounded kid. Unfortunately, the kid gets beat in the end. That's part of the motif, you understand.

Meanwhile, I enjoyed a small windfall. My grandfather had left me about fifteen hundred dollars. It was meant for something nobler, but I immediately booked a flight to Amsterdam in order to further my education. I'd never been to Europe, and it sounded like there was some education to be had in Amsterdam. My brother thought it was a bully idea. Amsterdam sounded like fun, and he'd never been to Europe either. I'd found him noticeably more depressed on this most recent pass through town. He was brooding more about his homosexuality, and tended to blame a lot of his other troubles on it. His looks were starting to go as well. He was losing his hair and carrying weight from all the Cutty. The kid who had looked like a million dollars in jeans and a T-shirt only a couple of years before was beginning to look prematurely middle-aged. When he was in the dumps he would sometimes ask me, pathetically, "And when you have children, would you trust me to be alone with them?"

Europe was a hoot. I wasn't there long and wound up having to move up my flight after getting into an altercation at the youth hostel in Amsterdam. I didn't want to be on hand the next evening when those Eurotrash motherfuckers turned up again. They were Mediterranean types, Latin boys, and I figured they might try and cut me. They'd certainly given that impression when we were separated the night before.

I phoned my brother from JFK. That's when he told me about the Mafia guys coming over to pay him a visit that same night. The computer scam had blown up in their faces and they were sore. He really didn't know whether they were going to dust him on the spot or let him try to talk his way out of it.

His scheme probably was foolproof. It was only a freakish stroke of bad luck that put the kibosh on it all. Unknown to my brother, the FBI had been tailing these two dopey hoods because of some Audubon paintings they'd managed to steal along the way. So when my brother went down to Philadelphia to meet with these guys, he was suddenly under the purview of the FBI as well, and they probably put a tap on his phone and found out that way about the fancy scam. I don't know what role the hoods played in the scam, but everyone was busted, and these two low-rent thugs wanted to know how come.

My brother lost his job, of course. Presumably the roof came down on his associate in Baltimore, which would have been extra-ugly with a wife and kids on the scene. With a felony rap still outstanding, the FBI decided to take a serious interest in my brother, putting a tail on him, harassing him. I can just imagine some dumb bastard in a gray suit and fedora scoping him out as he played pool at the International Stud and hoping against hope that no one back at the agency would catch wind of his assignment. My brother's situation must now have been desperate. I know he declared bankruptcy around this time to get himself clear of his legitimate debts, but most of his debts were below board and had to be paid off or he would receive another visit, one he wouldn't walk away from.

For all the grief that had fallen on his shoulders, he remained good company, and we still went out together almost every night, to this bar or that. Then one night he said to me, in the responsible, older-brother tone of voice, that I should go to Jersey and look in on Mom and Dad. It had been a while, and they had phoned him up and given him a hard time about it, etc. In retrospect, he was getting me out of there. Things were going to hell fast, and he didn't need me around as a spectator.

As for Jersey, the debut performance of my return engagement chez Mom and Dad was a catastrophe, and I was up the next morning at four, hitchhiking to Vancouver Island, back to college. On a pass through the region I had picked up an admission form at the University of Victoria, filled it out, and left it with the gal behind the desk. Somewhat to my surprise, they accepted me straightaway. So I had that as a backup. It certainly wasn't Plan A. And it struck me as more than a little bold to be standing on Palisade Avenue with my thumb out, headed for British Columbia, where I knew no-fuckingbody and had no reason to be. Then again, I had no alternative. I stuck out my thumb and waited. I didn't have to wait very long, really.

I spoke to my brother every few weeks, calling him collect (of course) from a pay phone around the corner from where I lived, a tiny basement flat belonging to a pleasant family called Galitzine, the head of which was a relation of the Russian tsars who cut a fine imperial figure and was given, on occasion, to theatrically imperial rages that I enjoyed through the ceiling.

It rained a lot that fall, sometimes in my room. But I was having a good time. It was something of a relief to be back in school, going to classes, reading the assigned literature. The regimentation was good for me after the chaos of the previous year. Also, I found it very pleasant to be around Canadian college girls. I had shed much of my shyness by then.

I'm not sure what the FBI thought they were onto with my brother. But they hounded him relentlessly those last few months, punitively, sadistically, it seemed. And they wouldn't have been the only ones. His IOUs would have been piling up at an alarming rate.

For all his low-life associations, he never had a gun, or even a proper knife you'd use to hurt someone. Goodness knows, we had grown up in a household where there would have been multiple deaths if a pistol had been available. Imagine growing up in America, in a neighborhood with gangsters, and as an adult having all those associations with gangsters, and still not having a gun. Exemplary, I would say. I remember wishing my brother had a gun when those two hoods came over. At least I could have shot a teenybopper or two before I got mine.

He was beginning to sound more and more gloomy when we spoke on the phone and had started sending signals, less and less vague, that he was making ready to check out. One time he talked about joining me out there in B.C., taking a job in a logging camp, getting back into shape, some good fresh air and all the rest. Well, I'd done a spot of logging work after arriving on the island and knew it wouldn't be his thing. He had a city boy's notion of going at a big tree with an axe, developing his biceps, playing cards at night with the guys. It was chainsaws and skidders and chokers: hard, shitty, dangerous work and with some of the stupidest motherfuckers on Planet Earth as your bunkmates. Heroin, too, the recreational drug of the B.C. logger: just what my brother needed.

One time I called him and told him about a party I'd been to the night before that had gotten a little out of hand and turned into a fuckathon. The idea of it was maybe more intoxicating than the event, but it was fun enough. This seemed to please him. He had always encouraged me to be more adventurous. When I told him about the party, it was as if I was telling the folks I had got all A-pluses on my report card. But I could also hear the sadness in his voice.

I don't know which phone call cinched it, when I knew he was going to go ahead. I remember telling him not to do anything "crazy" until I got back. He said something sweet to me, I forget. It was done.

He got the pills from his friend Bobby, a cute younger blond guy he'd tricked with over the years. I liked Bobby, but he was a part-time hustler and a congenital thief. They were friends, Bobby and my brother, but whenever Bobby came over he'd boost something. I guess my brother regarded it as a surcharge on the friendship. Maybe Bobby asked him what he needed fifty barbiturates for. He probably knew. Bobby was one of those relentlessly cheerful, optimistic souls, and completely unscrupulous.

I knew where it was all headed when I walked across the George Washington Bridge from Manhattan late that night. I'd missed the last bus. It's peaceful out in the middle, with the lights of the city at your back stretching south almost its entire length on your left and the Jersey Palisades in front of you, dark, in shadow but for a few lights. The river black, sheeny, two hundred feet below you.

I recalled an earlier crossing, walking home from a party in the city, or maybe a girl had thrown me out, I forget. I'd had a bellyful of hooch in me. There I was, approaching the middle of the bridge, headed for Jersey on the narrow walkway, and two young black guys, maybe sixteen or so, were headed my way from the opposite direction. Oh, shit, I thought to myself. Here's a chance to toss Whitey in the drink and no one'll ever find out. I'm aggressive when drunk and dumber than usual, and I figured my time had come. I was staring right at them now as they approached. As soon as one of them reached in his pocket, I figured, was when I'd make my move, maybe my last. The poor kids' eyes got big as saucers: What are we doing out here with this crazy drunk white motherfucker? was what their looks seemed to say.

I'll spare you the funeral and mourning rituals. It was pretty horrible. The spectacle of a parent grieving for a child is tough to watch, especially when it's your own parent. There was an animal sound coming out of my mother, like a dog wailing, but softer. I'd never seen a corpse up close before. I wasn't real thrilled that the first one belonged to my brother. Then there was the makeup and his icy-cold cheek.

I'm not big on religious expression unless the music is preternaturally good. The rabbi was a loathsomely unctuous character, most of them are. I told him he didn't know jack shit about my brother and to make it short or I'd make a scene. He obliged, but gave me one of those pitying looks.

You know how they have big get-togethers after, all of these ugly old dirtbags shaking their heads, tsk, tsk, tsk, drinking scotch and stuffing their faces with corned-beef sandwiches. That didn't sit well with me either. Then the phone rings. I'm hiding in the kitchen at the time. I pick it up and there is a tentative, shaky voice on the other end, almost like long distance. He identifies himself as John, a friend of my brother's. I never met John, or maybe once in passing at a bar. I seem to remember a face as I write this. John was my brother's major love. I'm not sure how long it lasted. Given my brother's nature and the nature of that whole scene, it couldn't have been more than a year or so. But John was the important one. John wasn't a trick. So I told John who I was and that I knew about him and my brother, and he just starts weeping and carrying on, telling me how much he loved him. It all started getting me going again. Most of the people who really loved my brother didn't come to the funeral because they didn't want to upset and embarrass everyone: you know, a bunch of weeping queers ruining it for everyone else.

When I returned to Victoria in January there was a long suicide note spread all over the floor of my little basement room. The kids upstairs must have gotten into it, the older of the boys only fourteen or so. I don't know whether they read it, but if they did it must have bewildered or frightened them.

Mostly it was a lot of "I'm sorry, I love you," along with instructions: key under the doormat, call the police, and so forth. There were a couple of guys, he wrote, who owed him money. He wanted me to make sure they ponied up. Some family stuff. Brotherly counsel. You'll get over it in time, etc. You can imagine what these things read like after the fact. I saved it for a long time, taking it out of my drawer to read every couple of years or so. Then I tossed it.

The aftermath, once I was back in Victoria, wasn't too bad. It was good to be four thousand miles away, to be sure. I vibrated a bit, like a guitar that's been struck by a blunt object, but even that calmed down over time, unless I smoked pot. I more or less had to quit smoking pot. Making love helped, and there was a girl or two on hand to oblige me. I suppose there's not much mystery in that: a little affection, a warm body to hold on to.

My professors had somehow gotten wind of it and treated me with kid gloves. It couldn't have been easy for a couple of them whom I went out of my way to irritate, but they tried. Even Basil Bunting, the visiting English poet whom I revered but whose criticism was merciless, found a couple of encouraging things to say about a poem of mine, but it simply wasn't in him to be insincere for more than one poem.

Before too long I was in a serious relationship, one that lasted seven years. I had made new friends. Every so often someone from back East would send me a message of commiseration or a note gently suggesting that maybe I should see a psychiatrist and talk things over. Both sorts of communication drove me into a rage.

One of the things my brother was most afraid of was becoming a "pathetic old queen," as he put it. Like many good-looking young males, champion athletes, golden youths, he wasn't destined to age well. People would say to me, "Too bad about your brother." Fuck 'em, what do they know about it? I never begrudged him what he did. He was in a lot of pain. A lot of people seem to think you're on this earth to keep them amused. It never made me love him less or think less of him. If you ask me, it took guts. Most people simply hold on to life and rot.

I used to go visit him in the city when he still lived in Chelsea, not long after he'd moved to town. I was finishing high school. Maybe a couple of times a year, no more, I'd take the train downtown from the Bronx instead of going back to Jersey. I was wretchedly unhappy at school and at being sixteen, and I would confess to him all my anxieties, all my perceived failings and inadequacies. I couldn't have made for very thrilling company. But he always acted glad to see me. He never put me down or pulled a disapproving face. "You'll be all right, lover boy," he'd say, smiling. "Let's go out and see if we can't find ourselves a drink." I miss having someone like that in my life. I miss it like a limb.